Church and Gender Justice

Reimagining Church as Event: Perspectives from the Margins
Series Editors: George Zachariah and Sudipta Singh

In these eleven volumes, a collective of Indian theologians envisions Church as an Event that happens in particular contexts in the life of the communities at the margins. They argue that in the life of the communities who experience on their bodies the violence and hegemony of dominant power relations, morality, and religious dogmas and practices, the church happens as countercultural experiences that disrupt the logic of the prevailing order. These experiences enable and empower them to affirm and celebrate their differences, knowledges and beauty even as they weave their liberation. Church as event is a call to rising to life, creating life-flourishing communities that live out the foretaste of the reign of God.

Titles in this Series

Church and Religious Diversity Joshua Samuel and Samuel Mall
Church and Gender Justice Aruna Gnanadason
Faith in the Age of Empire Y.T. Vinayaraj
Dalitekklesia: A Church from Below Raj Bharath Patta
Church and Climate Justice Vinod Wesley
Church and Disability Samuel George
Church and Diakonia in the Age of COVID-19 Mothy Varkey
Decolonising Oikoumene Gladson Jathanna
Church and Human Sexuality Arvind Theodore
With Many Voices: Liturgies in Context Viji Varghese Eapen (Ed.)
The Word Becoming Flesh George Zachariah

Church and Gender Justice

Aruna Gnanadason

2020

Church and Gender Justice - jointly published by the Indian Society for Promoting Christian Knowledge (ISPCK), Post Box 1585, Kashmere Gate, Delhi-110006 and Council for World Mission, Singapore-338729.

ISBN: 978-93-88945-77-6

Kindle Edition: 978-93-88945-89-9

Cover Picture Credit : Immanuel Paul Vivekanandh K

Laser typeset by

ISPCK, Post Box 1585, 1654, Madarsa Road, Kashmere Gate, Delhi-110006 • *Tel:* 23866323

e-mail: ashish@ispck.org.in • ella@ispck.org.in
website: www.ispck.org.in

*This book was made possible through
the kind contribution of the Council for World Mission*

Contents

Foreword

DISCERNMENT AND RADICAL ENGAGEMENT (DARE) is an initiative of the Council for World Mission (CWM) to enable faith communities to *clarify what it means to engage in* public witness to God's justice and peace in a corrupt and conflicted world.

> The mission of DARE is conceived as the coming together of (a) the *radical soul* of discernment and sense-making in theology and biblical criticism; (b) the yearnings for *signifying engagement* that rise out of the slums of modernism and the valleys of despair; and (c) the commitment to redemption songs that *inspire disturbance* at the hubs of power.

As part of the DARE initiative, each region of CWM is invited to prepare and share biblical and theological resources on current themes and issues being considered by CWM, drawing upon the experiences and resources from the region.

Interfaith Engagement, Ecumenism and Inclusive communities against dehumanising social categorisations are the themes for the book series undertaken by the South Asia region of CWM. The thrust is centred on **Reimagining Church as Event: Perspectives from the Margins**. It calls to the fore persons living in the margins and highlights their voice, their narratives and their passion for a rearrangement of life in communities, as we know it, and a commitment to rise to life and to break out from Babylon. These books are intended for the use of lay people, pastors and evangelists as well as for theological students and seminaries. The series offer stories and narratives, analyses, liturgical resources, biblical, theological and ethical reflections, and missional/praxis proposals.

Church is an event that happens at the margins of contemporary life. Church happens as an epiphanic event where the divine presence is manifested and experienced in the pathos, struggles, contestations and harmonies of everyday existence. Church happens in those spaces where we celebrate the presence of Jesus, the Christ, in the flourishing of life. Church happens when we are transformed by one another, and inspired and enabled to engage in the transformative politics of the reign of God. Church happens whenever and wherever spirit-filled communities reclaim their subversive moral agency and contest the logic and practices of domination and exclusion. Church happens when the community experiences the healing power of the wounded healer and join Jesus in this risk-taking mission, despite the wounds we bear. To reimagine Church requires courage and commitment to engage in the mission of nurturing and organising communities of resistance and healing. This book series is a humble attempt at exposing and encouraging this radical expression of Church.

I appreciate and thank all those who are associated with this series, the authors, the contributors, the publishers and the editors. I commend this book series in the hope and prayers that they will help the faith communities in South Asia, and beyond, to *discern God's presence in community and dare to engage* in ways that re-present the God of life in communities and in the public square, *Rising to Life: Living out the New Heaven and New Earth.*

Colin Cowan
General Secretary
Council for World Mission

Introduction

*Philip Vinod Peacock**

The issue of Gender discrimination is something that haunts our communities, our churches and our church-based institutions. National Crime Records inform us that in the year 2006 two women were reported as being raped every hour, of course we are well aware of the number of cases that do not go reported and the number of cases that cannot be reported. Sure numbers such as these should perhaps suggest to us the scale of the issue. Rape and sexual assault are crimes that are not about sex but are really about power and domination. Rape and the threat of rape therefore are really about the reinforcement of patriarchal values and the control of women through the use of violence and its threat. Sexual assault against women also engages and interconnects with other factors such as class, caste, communalism and ethnicity so that the locations of violence caused by these other factors are on the body of the woman. Even further we find that it is often the woman who is blamed for rape itself. Statements like 'she invited it' or 'it was the clothes she was wearing' only serve to blame the victim for her victimization and shift the attention away from the aggressor. Even in situations where there is no overt blaming of the victim, society organizes itself in such a way that it directs its attention to women when we deal with the issue of rape, so we 'over protect' our daughters rather than train our sons into healthy sexualities. In fact the only time we speak to our men about rape and sexual assault is in terms of their 'protection' of women and girls. Though rape is an issue that is extremely relevant and pertinent to our communities and society it is not one that finds its place in the context of our institutions and colleges, even our theological colleges. We seldom hear of any discussion on this issue in our places of work or study.

And while we cannot deny that rape and a culture of rape is very much prevalent in our contexts, we should be equally aware that sexual harassment is rampant.. Sexual harassment, is intimidation, bullying, teasing or coercion of a sexual nature, or the unwelcome or inappropriate promise of rewards in exchange for sexual favors. It involves the telling of lewd jokes to women or the showing of pornography to women, or the passing of comments. The question is how are we addressing this issue? It would do us well to remind ourselves that by government regulations we need to have a sexual harassment committee in our churches and church institutions that offer rights and means of redressal to the victims of these offences.

But Gender discrimination at the workplace and educational institution works beyond the active violence of women and is embedded into the structure itself. It is found in the subtle discouragement of women in education and employment. It is found in the feminization of certain subjects and the overt masculinization of the Science, Technology, Engineering and Maths streams, or what has come to be called STEM. It is found in the policing of women's bodies through rules restricting their movement and the way that they choose to dress themselves, suggesting that controlling their sexuality is more important than their education. It is further found in the incorrect theology that women can only find their salvation through marriage and childbirth and that right from the birth of a girl efforts are taken to prepare her for marriage and family life.

So, what are we to do? Obviously, there is a lot of work to be done, at the global, national, church and local level. There may be and even must be other occasions to talk about this. I am just going to restrict myself to our community here and am only going to restrict myself to three things I am going to suggest. The first is that we must commit to being feminist and to looking at the world through a feminist gaze. But what is a feminist gaze? I believe that it is necessarily two things, firstly it is the revealing of the strenuous, complex of power equations which goes on below the surface of what looks normal, smooth and complete. Among the Christian community we live in the illusion that we are a progressive space which offers opportunities for women, and maybe to an extent we are, but what we need to do is to occupy a feminist gaze which would expose the dominant male forces and would challenge that which we perceive as natural and normal. A second thing that a feminist gaze would do is to call us to occupy the margins of every situation, that we look at and analyze what is happening from the perspective of those who are left out, those who do not speak and those who are crushed into silence. In this sense what we must realize is that just because a strong critique is not emerging is not evidence we are in a just space, but it just may mean that voices are not allowed to emerge at all.

The second is that we must actively commit to enabling the women of our institutions is to be able to form a collective which will regularly meet where it is hoped that issues pertaining to them will emerged. One of the ways of strengthening patriarchy is through resisting the organization of women. We must buck this trend and we need to have active and perhaps also politically engaged women's organization. And we need to listen to the voices that emerge out of this collective of women. Perhaps this is our sin, that we do not just allow women not to speak, but when they speak we refuse to listen, believing that we know what is best for them. A collective women's voice can work to drown this enforced silence and will perhaps work towards women's voices being listened to. Unfortunately, women's collectives in our institutions are often reduced to charity or cooking thus blunting a potential political edge that this organizations of women can actually take. This is something we need to be careful of.

Thirdly we must begin to engage men and particularly male pastors and male theological students with questions of gender justice. We have to begin to see how we can re-socialize men into redemptive masculinities, how men can contribute to gender justice. It is a matter of personal sadness to me when I see the men sniggering about gender justice and getting all insecure whenever the women come together as a collective. What we must understand is that patriarchy is not God's design for the world and to believe so is to fall short of Jesus' demand for discipleship.

Endotes

* **The Rev. Philip Vinod Peacock** serves the World Communion of Reformed Churches as Executive Secretary for Justice and Witness.

Chapter 1

Patriarchy and Gender Constructions Exposed

Patriarchy Defined

There have been many definitions of patriarchy—this is because as a system it operates differently in different contexts. In classical terms, "patriarchy" literally means "rule of the father in a male-dominated family." Patriarchy in all times, ancient to the present, is recognised as the foundation on which family and society have been built. In all of Asia, and particularly in South Asia, patriarchy coexists with and is buttressed by religions and cultures. One thing remains a constant in all religions and communities in this region—patriarchy rules! There are a few pockets where matriarchy (or the rule of the mother) exists, but in most places patriarchal values and power have all but submerged family systems based on matriarchy and the alternate values matriarchy offers in terms of relationships and power equations.

In a bid to be faithful to reflect on the experiences of patriarchy for all women in South Asia we are likely to fall into the trap of abstract universalisms. The universal values we claim as our understanding of the impact of patriarchal injustice is often based on Western scholarship and categories. But then, to keep our discussions rooted in Asia is a challenge as there is no "one South Asian woman" or "one South Asian reality that defines patriarchy." This word of caution comes particularly in the context of emerging cultural national chauvinism that is the trend in most South Asian countries. Women's rights are on the edges of this discussion, even if (excepting for a few outspoken but fringe ideologues) no one in power really speaks out strongly against the atrocities meted out to women (and other minorities)—often in the name of protecting "national pride" and the so-called "national culture."

Vahida Nainar writes:

Patriarchal notions of male dominance are also reinforced through religion and culture. The conservatives in all the countries of South Asia espouse a rigid and fundamentalist understanding and interpretation of religion and culture that promote male domination and women's subordination as a virtue. The practice of punishing a woman for adultery in the event of a rape in Afghanistan and Pakistan is justified as Islamic, but in fact has its basis in cultural practices and attitudes. The treatment of a widow and the association of women as inauspicious and impure find a place in Hindu texts such as the Manusmriti. A cultural notion of South Asian women as demure and obedient in conduct and modest in appearance is still a basis for judging women's character as "good" and "bad."[1]

Ensuring the Male Line

In India, the Vedic period (1500-500 BC) is called the golden era for women in Indian society; ironically it is also the time when the caste system of graded subjugation was instituted.

There is evidence, from those times, that religious literature such as the Vedas dictate that a wife is particularly required to be under male control, and female sexuality is to be rigidly monitored with rules and regulations to ensure caste purity of children. Vahida Nainar states that "the practice in Afghanistan and Pakistan of punishing women for adultery if they are raped and cannot produce witnesses to the rape is based on the mortal fear of women's 'latent and explosive' sexuality that would run amok and would make it difficult to identify the father of these children. Women's sexuality has to belong to the man who can benefit from it at will, which is the underlying reason for the belief that there is no such thing as marital rape. With marriage the woman is supposed to have signed off the use of her body to her husband." [2]

Patrilineal succession has been upheld and has been handed down as the governing system from one generation to the next in a bid to control and retain private family property, and this includes the woman a man marries—she too becomes "his property". Such systems remain dominant until now in all South Asian societies, with restrictions of time, space and movement imposed on women to keep them in check. By and large, women are raised to believe that the home and its maintenance is their domain.

Vahida Nainar writes that almost all countries in this region (she names Afghanistan, Bangladesh, Bhutan, India, the Maldives, Nepal, Pakistan, Sri Lanka) are agrarian economies. Here,

> Women are kept mostly within the prescribed sphere of the private, i.e. at home, keeping it going, caring for the children

and elderly. Where women step out of their home to work in
the land, they often do so to produce subsistence value that is
consumed by the household. Modes of production are organized
in a manner where the family expropriates women's labour.[3]

In most parts of South Asia, men's role includes earning an
income to support a family and working in farms and in
factories, while the women's role includes the responsibility to
bear and care for children, run a household and to supplement
the family income also with a job. Running a household and
caring for children is not always considered a "full-time" job
and is unpaid work. Children are taught their specified roles
when they are very young.

Defining Gender Roles

Gender roles are not natural. They are formed by, and vary
within, society, culture, geographic location, politics and
time. People are programmed into certain gender roles and
social categories through socialisation and interaction with
others. There are many social agents that contribute to the
construction of gender roles. Parents and family are important
socialisation agents in the gender role development of children.
The school setting is another social agent. Schools often
separate children. Even the fact that most teachers are female
and most of the administration is male causes children to
realise that each gender has a different role in life. This kind
of treatment makes children grow up with the consciousness
that boys and girls must recognise power differentials between
them. The media is a powerful social agent that portrays gender
roles and stereotypes. Many prime-time television shows,
movies and commercials portray young beautiful women as

either sex symbols or the "typical" women who cook, clean and care for the house. These situations teach young girls that beauty (and this includes having a fair skin) and their role as nurturers are what is valued in society.

What is of interest is the role the church has played in this socialisation. Gender relations and roles permeate all levels of the church and is here too often based on the abuse of power by some. The church, when trying to address gender issues, must keep in mind that it could offer an alternative paradigm of partnership, even if it does not exist in isolation—we are dealing with a situation of imbalance that is found not only within its own walls but is pervasive in societies, cultures and histories. And yet, the church has to provide a healing voice of justice and equality as part of Christian mission, founded on a theology and spirituality that has as its basis inclusiveness and justice. What regretfully persists is that the church contributes to women's oppression by theologically justifying patriarchy. In order to build and sustain a healthy and thriving community of women and men, the church needs to nurture the understanding of the image of God as present in all its members—men, women, and those of many sexual orientations. In order to serve justice and dignity to all that this community requires of us, we need to be engaged in a constant process of learning and unlearning beliefs, attitudes.

Of course, it is not only women who are trained and taught to behave in particular expected and required ways. Men too are systematically trained and socialised into some forms of (even toxic) behaviour—the understanding that "boys must be boys" and that the use of force and violence is the way to exert power if the man is to play his role effectively as the one in control, are values that boys are taught and imbibe as they grow up. Men who wish to display an alternative pattern of behaviour, to be more caring and nurturing and refusing to use force to exert influence, are mocked and critiqued cruelly and called "henpecked" or "sissy". The differential training of girls and boys leads to gender imbalance and even to violence.

As our societies grow there are new developments in sex roles. The male world has expanded and men have the opportunity to take up new careers and the freedom to move around more conveniently. They are still the breadwinners and dominate not just the private sector but also the government, legal and service agencies. Women's roles during this time have also changed but not as much as that of men. Women's primary role is still as homemaker and childcare provider even if millions of women have also entered the workforce. Even now, in many jobs, women are paid considerably less than men and have in addition an "unpaid" role as housewives. However, it must be acknowledged that there are changes today in the work women are doing, and in some contexts, men have recognised the talents women bring to the career world—men have no choice but to accept women. Fortunately, at the same time, more and more men feel liberated and are taking on roles that were once deemed 'female', like nursing, homemaking and teaching.

Restricting the control of women's sexuality within the family has been expanded to society and has become "a social and ideological construct which considers men (who are the patriarchs) as superior to women."[4] Suranjita Roy speaks of it as a system of power relations which are hierarchical and unequal where men control women's production, reproduction and sexuality. "It imposes masculinity and femininity character stereotypes in society which strengthen the iniquitous power relations between men and women."[5]

Sigmund Freud, the psychoanalyst, is famously to have said that "anatomy is destiny," implying that it is women's biology that primarily defines not just women's roles but their abilities and skills! It is important to recognise that feminists do accept and acknowledge that biological differences might lead to some differences in roles, **but** it cannot become the basis for sexual hierarchy in which males assume dominance or the power to determine that some roles have less value and therefore can be trivialised. Pierre Bourdieu, a professor in social sciences in France, has written an excellent treatise debunking Freud's position. He claims that it is not biological reproduction that determines the division of labour and of the whole natural and social order, but "it is an arbitrary construction of the male and female body, its uses and functions, especially in biological reproduction, which gives an apparently natural foundation to the androcentric view of the division of sexual labour."[6]

Violence against Women to Enforce Obedience to Patriarchal Power

The most outrageous forms of violence are perpetrated against women and girls in all South Asian countries. Most often, violence against women is a tool to enforce patriarchy. Women are unsafe on the streets, in institutions of higher learning, in their homes and even in places of religious worship. The reasons for violence in the home are most often trivial—it could be tasteless food; suspicion of adultery; disobedience to the orders of the man; violating norms of family honour, for example, in the event of a woman wanting to marry a person of another religion or caste group. Violence can be subtle to life-threatening—breaking patriarchal codes and expectations can be the instigation for violent retaliation.

Violence against women till recently was not viewed as a human rights violation, and till now most people have viewed women's rights as domestic, relating to the family and as personal. Therefore, gross violations such as rape; domestic violence leading to death; trafficking in women and sexual slavery; sexual harassment in the workplace (and in churches and its institutions); and the abuse of women's bodies and sexuality in the media have all been viewed as private and therefore not deserving public dialogue and action. It is a fact that women are not considered worthy of focused attention—in the eyes of most people they are not fully human—unless they are viewed in the context of a particular man, family, clan or tribe.

The murder of women in their homes is reported every now and then—in 1999, at least 1,000 women were murdered in Pakistan and 90 per cent of women there reported being subject to gender based violence. Law enforcement authorities routinely dismiss domestic violence as private disputes. With this form of violence, it is important to acknowledge that marital rape is not considered a crime in most countries in this region. Most women do not report the abuse they experience because they want to avoid ruining their family's reputation, they are scared the abuse will get worse, and they are afraid they would be separated from their husband and children. Women who do report abuse are often harassed by the police and their families. It is a known fact that about 33 per cent of women who are victims of physical abuse do not file complaints. When it comes to marital abuse, even pregnant women can be victims. Some women enter religious communities or religious events to avoid being at home and face further violence. Some ask for help from their friends and family, but most are reluctant to make formal complaints because they feel they would not be understood. Women who report rape or sexual assault by strangers are often disbelieved and treated with disrespect by abusive police personnel and other law enforcement officials. Forensic doctors focus on a battered woman's status rather than on her injuries. Most often, women also have to deal with reluctant or sceptical judges. The police in Pakistan often refuse to record the complaint of women when an officer may have been involved.[7]

Regretfully, such attitudes are reinforced and given divine justification by all our religions, including Christianity, as it is taught to us. The church and Christianity have relegated women to second-class citizenship, even in the life and ministry of the church Token positions of leadership for women (apart from a few exceptions) are still the order of the day. Women rarely make it into higher political positions unless they have the backing of a family or a man. A few women have managed to make it into leadership positions in the corporate world by "breaking what is called the glass ceiling" or the invisible walls that block the movement of women within institutional structures; and a few women have begun their own small businesses—but then on the other side there are "underground realities" of women who are domestic workers, street cleaners, manual scavengers, tea pickers and those who do what is considered "the less important" farming tasks. Asian women, who are said to be non-aggressive, docile and pliable, have been forced into prostitution or are sought out for domestic work. Millions of women in South Asia continue to live demeaning lives, doing work which does not fit the category of what the International Labour Organisation (ILO) has termed "decent work."[8]

Desire, sexuality and sexual choices are determined and controlled by patriarchal norms within the strict parameters of marriage and family. "For women, the domain of the family is the most intimate and the most difficult within which to exercise their autonomy. In a reality that rarely extends beyond the limited universe of the household, the family becomes the primary source of affirmation of women.... Motherhood therefore is not merely a personal aspiration, but often a means to social recognition. Such expectations alienate and oppress single women, widows and barren women and encourage prejudice reinforced by culture and religion."[9]

Education of the Girl Child

According to UNICEF, an estimated 11.3 million children of primary school age (5.8 million girls and 5.5 million boys) and 20.6 million children of lower-secondary school age (8.9 million girls and 11.6 million boys) in South Asia do not go to school. In Bangladesh, for instance, 40 per cent of secondary-school-age adolescent girls are out of school and are vulnerable to violence and abuse, including child marriage, child labour, drug addiction and physical and psychological violence. This is leading to the highest incidence of child marriage and child labour in the world. Only about half of the primary-aged children receive an education with minimum learning standards. Clearly, we also have a **learning crisis** in South Asia. Many classrooms are still characterised by teacher-centred rote learning. Many pupils are also victims of corporal punishment and discrimination. And when we look at **young people**, only a quarter of them leave school with the skills they need. This growing gap in skills will stunt economic growth, with far-reaching social and political repercussions. UNICEF has set a target of ensuring that 10 million out-of-school boys and girls are enrolled in and learning in pre-primary, primary and secondary schools by 2021. In the present environment will this goal be reached?[10]

Religious Nationalism and Control of Women

Today, with the rising power of religious fundamentalism and cultural nationalism, Christian women (and other minorities) are placed in an even more vulnerable position. The fact that Christian women (nuns, for example) have been the target of attack and violence as acts of retribution on the Christian community is documented if one scans through reports in the past few years. Moral policing of women is also an outcome of the new "cultural nationalism." Random acts of violence against women for being "improperly" dressed does happen particularly in urban centres and among women in universities or the workforce.

There is an undermining of cultural diversity and a refusal to learn from the wisdom of those who are organising themselves into people's movements to make the environment safe; their ways of life have meaning for the future of our peoples and for safeguarding democracy and constitutional values (an example is the mass peaceful movement of Muslim women in all the big cities in India protesting against a discriminatory law, enacted in December 2019, which demands proof of citizenship[11]). Recognition of liberation strands in the life and witness of subaltern communities—Dalits, Indigenous peoples and, in this case, Muslim women—is yet to gain ascendency in an age that thrives on profit and the exploitation of peoples against a backdrop of religious bigotry.

Laws and Anti-girl-child Policies

Women's education has been underplayed and not invested in by these countries because by and large the dominant mindset is that since childbearing and rearing are the main goals for women's lives education would be wasted on them. Keeping women in the lowest paid jobs ensures women's total dependency on men. Systematic son preference has manifested itself in sex-selective elimination of female foetuses, giving rise to skewed male-female sex ratios. The last census in India, for example, recorded 914 females per 1,000 males, down from 927 per 1,000 in the 2001 Census.

Comparisons among South Asian countries (excluding Afghanistan, Bhutan and the Maldives) indicate several important regional patterns. First, the Muslim advantage in sex ratios seems to be pronounced in South Asian countries.

In 2011, India's Muslim-majority neighbours, Pakistan and Bangladesh, largely possessed normal child sex ratios. Bangladesh has had a historic fall in fertility in the last three decades from 6 to 2.2 children per woman. Nevertheless, Bangladesh has also simultaneously substantially improved sex ratios from 1990 to the current 982 females for every 1,000 males. Despite the disclosure of the sex of the foetus (since it is not banned with ultrasound technology) in Bangladesh the practice of sex-selective abortion is "almost entirely absent," as abortions themselves are illegal.[12]

Additionally, many other laws and policies buttress patriarchy in South Asia. The example is given of how the conservatives in the Afghanistan parliament defeated a bill on the Elimination of Violence Against Women which sought to abolish child marriage and eliminate the prevailing practice of charging women for adultery in the event of rape! Lawmakers argued that removing the latter practice would lead to social chaos—women would indulge in extramarital relationships safe in the knowledge that there would be no consequences. A similar law called the Hudood Ordinance was passed by the Zia-ul-Haq government in Pakistan in 1980.[13]

We live in a region trapped in the unjust and ruthless pursuit of economic growth at all costs, ensuring scandalous levels of poverty of which women and girls are the primary victims, and their gender in interaction with caste and ethnicity make them the most vulnerable section of the population. Change is slow because any number of reforms or small expressions of success do not make any real difference. Unjust and biased economic systems thrive in creating wealth for a small percentage of the people and poverty for millions — systems that are in essence patriarchal and anti-poor. For example, the media, which could be a powerful social agent of change, is embedded in the hands of a few business houses or multinational industries and only aids and abets the portrayal of women's bodies and sexuality in ways that will draw profits while adding to the threats against women. Even women's organised power is unable to withstand various forms of economic abuse of women's sexuality.

While expectations about appropriate gender role characteristics and sexual behaviour have evolved throughout history, especially for women and sexual minorities, there is still a strong relationship between the social construction of gender and compulsory heterosexuality. Homophobia runs rife in our societies in South Asia because our sexuality and sexual choices have been determined by what is considered "natural", and lesbian, gay, transsexual, bisexual or transgendered women, and queer women, are dismissed as engaging in "unnatural sex"—by societies, churches and, unfortunately, some women's movements too in the church and society.

Women in the Public Sphere in South Asia

All the countries in this region have a long heritage of women's presence in the public sphere. To give the example of India, one major figure and movement from the late nineteenth century is worth highlighting. Savitribai Phule, along with her reformer husband, struggled against the caste system and for the right to education for Dalits and women. They also raised issues concerning all women in India—education of the girl child, abolishment of the purdah and widow remarriage. There was women's participation in the Ambedkarite movement as well as in Periyar's "Self-Respect Movement" in Tamil Nadu in 1925. Worth mentioning is the organisation of women within the Telangana peasant struggle in the mid-1940s. Women had also been part of the freedom struggle under the leadership of Mahatma Gandhi, who saw the participation of women in the non-violent form of resistance as being particularly effective. From then through the 1970s to date women have continued to play an active and courageous role in public life.

Rakshinda Perveen, a journalist, writes:

South Asia has had eminent women politicians and office bearers. The world's first woman prime minister was from Sri Lanka who was elected in 1960. The first woman prime minister of the Muslim world was from Pakistan and was elected twice. Bangladesh, Nepal and India have had women head of the states as well. Maldives is an exception as women are banned from holding the highest leadership positions of president and vice-president in the country. Afghanistan is a new democracy and has reached 28 percent in terms of women representation in the parliament. Nepal is the only South Asian country that has 33 percent women legislators. In spite of this legacy, the authority of a vast majority of South Asian women as voters and leaders remains a distant dream.

The women in politics in South Asia, like elsewhere, have to face patriarchal attitudes and arrangements. They usually receive limited support from civil society groups and seasoned parliamentarians in politics. The framework of the electoral system may not always match the needs of the women candidates. The exposition of shrewd patriarchal accord among political parties is not incomprehensible. Those who run for the seat frequently materialise it through the boost and the blessings of their godfathers and pedigree.[14]

For example, in Pakistan, all the most powerful women have come to power because of family patronage—Fatima Jinnah, Syeda Safia Begum, Benazir Bhutto (who was the first female Prime Minister of Pakistan).

Bangladesh has the eighth lowest gender gap in political empowerment in the world. This is partially due to the fact that it has had a female head of state for longer than any other country in the world. In addition, the proportion of seats held by women in the national parliament doubled from 10 per cent in 1990 to 20 per cent in 2011. Women's growing presence in the political sphere has had important implications on the family structure. Society is moving away from the traditional view that women are an economic liability and that sons are more desirable than daughters. Studies show that the growing independence of women is one of the major causes for a decline in the "missing women" phenomenon i.e. gender-based infanticide in Bangladesh.

Despite the fact that women do not generally have ownership of land and tools necessary for agriculture, their labour has been a vital part of the success Bangladesh has had in agricultural productivity; the country stands out in comparison with other countries in Asia in terms of agricultural productivity. In addition, Bangladesh has experienced significant improvements in women's health over the past three decades. Women's life expectancy, for example, increased from 54.3 years in 1980 to 69.3 years in 2010, one of the largest increases in the region. Begum Rokeya, Sheikh Hasina (the current Prime Minister of Bangladesh), Khaleda

Zia and Begum Matia Chowdhury are some prominent women in Bangladesh's political history.

In Sri Lanka, female representation is as low as below 6 per cent in the national legislature, and despite over 51 per cent of the Sri Lankan population constituting women, their low representation in policymaking bodies is of concern. The percentage of women holding seats in parliament (as of 2013) was 5.8 per cent, which is a lot less than in Nepal (33.2 per cent), Bangladesh (19.7 per cent) and India (10.9 per cent). Stereotypical notions about the 'right' place for women in society is one of the reasons why women are reluctant to play a major role in Sri Lankan politics. Hampered by the social norms surrounding the 'role of a woman,' most females lack the required level of competence and political knowledge to run a successful election campaign on par with male candidates. This is quite tragic, considering the active roles that many women play in their communities through volunteering and various social service activities.

In a context where female graduates in universities outnumber males, and in a context where access to education and skills development is comparatively higher for a woman than a decade back, few women succeed in the field of politics. Discrimination occurs within the political parties themselves. However much their manifestos talk about empowering women and increasing their participation, all parties are prejudiced against female candidates. Although 74per cent of the people believe that women should be in politics, they also believe that politics is "not the right place" for women. Most political parties are reluctant to give nominations to females as they feel it would be a 'waste' to nominate a candidate who may not win. There are deep-rooted stereotypes within political parties. Even if a woman is elected to the parliament, they are hardly considered for ministerial portfolios other than those related directly to women. In fact, many political parties encourage their female candidates to talk about women's empowerment in their political campaigns, while the male candidates are encouraged to speak on much 'broader' issues. According to this line of thinking, women are not competent to handle any other subject than those related to women's own issues.[15] Three of the most prominent women who have been in power in Sri Lanka are Adeline Molamure, Sirimavo Bandaranaike and Chandrika Kumaratunga.

Indira Gandhi was the strongest female Indian politician and a central figure in national politics in India. She was the first and, to date, the only female Prime Minister of India. She served as Prime Minister from January 1966 to March 1977 and again from January 1980 until her assassination in October 1984, making her the second longest-serving Indian Prime Minister. In recent times we have had two or three powerful women participate boldly in parliamentary debates, but by and large Rashida Perveen is right when she concludes that, "Women regardless of their eloquence have negligible say during discussions on important matters within their political parties. The women legislators thrive as male proxy and their power extension."[16]

To go back to the history of women in public life, the 1970s saw a new awakening of women, which was referred to as the second wave of the women's movement in many parts of South Asia. Rape, price rise of basic goods, right to access to water, increasing domestic violence and legal rights of women were the main issues on the agenda at that time. Feminist activists are often told until now that "feminism is a Western product" that is alien to Asia—this in spite of the contribution women have made to bring in alternatives in every field of political life.

Today we once too often hear the claim that Christianity too is a Western product—so it is a challenge how we should position ourselves as Christian feminists in the public sphere. Flavia Agnes has dealt with this dilemma in an article[17] where she regrets that "secularism" as an ideology was never specifically articulated or discussed by the feminist movement. She writes that religion was in the 1970s and 1980s considered largely to be a private and suspiciously superstitious affair. She describes how her 'secular' Hindu friends had been wary of this, considering it as religious backwardness, and not seeing the parallels between Flavia's identification with cultural Christianity and their own cultural Hinduism.[18] Flavia's suggestion for the way forward into the future is for the feminist movement today to, rather than believe and assume that it is secular, actually become secular more intentionally.[19]

It is only in recent years that communal identities of women, or caste divides for that matter, have reared their ugly heads. In the past decades these divides were largely ignored—those in the women's movement believed that they were all primarily women, and it was this identity around which they organised themselves. Urvashi Butalia acknowledges that:

> In feminist circles I had barely considered that there could be something other than their interest as women that could hold women together. The complexity of their roles, the difficulties of struggle given these, were absent from much of our discussions. That women's loyalties could have shifted, that they were not undifferentiated and homogeneous, that their interests could tie in with those of their men and their class— these dimensions are important for feminists to question and understand.[20]

In India the 1992 riots (Mumbai) and since then other incidents of communal violence (including Gujarat's Godhra in 2002 and Odisha's Khandamal in 2008) and other recent religious tensions and violence since the government decided to institute a National Population Register and other similar laws that have particularly targeted the citizenship of Muslims in the country have influenced the women's movement, which now recognises the importance of religious identity in the public sphere.

Given the complexity of women's movements in South Asia and the way women have had to negotiate their way through the maze of patriarchy, there is a problem in the way Third World (here Asian) women are sometimes constructed by women in the West. It is not possible to speak of all women in one category. Essentialism tends to make some women's historical subordination to men and to other women seem like a natural fact rather than as a cultural, economic and political product. "Overemphasis on individualistic female subjectivity may sometimes overshadow other power dynamics."[21] As Radhika Coomaraswamy, from Sri Lanka, who was the United Nation's Special Rapporteur on Violence Against Women puts it, "The tension between the universality of human rights and cultural relativism is particularly complex, as women's identities are so integrally linked to their culture and community; women are thus wary of critical outsiders."[22]

What Laura Donaldson, a native American feminist, writes for her context is true for Asia too: "As we have seen, many feminist discussions overlook the material specificity of gender and assign women's place within gender ideology according to the machinations of an a-historical patriarchy. If Marxism ignores the gender-saturated nature of all class-relations, then feminism ignores the racially saturated nature of all gender relations."[23] It is therefore important to acknowledge the power of the women's movement, in each context, in even the most patriarchal cultures, which is on its own power negotiating and sometimes fighting against cultural relations that reveal themselves in violent expressions against women.

An appeal to Christian Anthropology as a Response to Patriarchy and Systems of Graded Subjugation

To bring to a close this chapter that gives an overview of how patriarchy and gender operate in South Asia, I appeal to Christian anthropology to move us beyond. A meditation written at the Pre-Assembly Pan-Orthodox Churches meeting held in Antelias, Lebanon, in January 2005 speaks powerfully of our creation as men and women. The prayer goes thus:

O merciful God
Out of Your own loving-kindness, in Your grace.
You have created the world in which You were well pleased.
You made us, human beings,

Whom You endowed with Your own image, after Your own likeness....

But we have abused our freedom,

We have distorted Your image,

and became alienated from Your living presence...

The necessity to speak of patriarchy and gender arises out of a basic discrepancy and a turning away from the will of God as defined in the Scriptures, leading to a situation where genders are often treated as if they are unequal. The imperative to act on patriarchy and gender issues is an integral part of the mission of the churches because, as Christians, we believe that in community all are equal participants in the Body of Christ. The implications of our mutual partaking in the divine image and in Christ's body are deep; this has to be done with mutual love, respect, and an attention to each other's God-given dignity as we live together in this world. Hospitality, justice and compassion, care, respect and honour all follow from our being created "in the image of God."

Endnotes

[1] Vahida Nainar, "Patriarchy in South Asia, Structures and Relations," in *Analyse and Kritik,* June 2013. https://papers.ssrn.com/sol3/papers.cfm?abstract_id=2317080 Accessed 1 March 2020.

[2] Ibid.

[3] Vahida Nainar, "Patriarchy in South Asia," 2013.

[4] Suranjita Ray. http://www.du.ac.in/fileadmin/DU/Academics/course_material/hrge_06.pdf Accessed 7 March 2020.

[5] Suranjita Ray. 2020.

[6] Pierre Bourdieu, Prelude, *Masculine Domination*, (Stanford, California: Stanford University Press, 2001), 23.

[7] https://en.wikipedia.org/wiki/Women_in_Pakistan. Accessed 15 Feb 2020

[8] https://en.wikipedia.org/wiki/Decent_work. Accessed 15 Feb 2020.

[9] Monica Melanchthon, "The Song of Songs," in *The Global Bible Commentary* ed. Daniel Patte et al. (Nashville: Abingdon 2004), 180.

[10] www.unicefrosa-progressreport.org/childeducation.html. Data from various UN sources Accessed 15 Feb 2020.

[11] https://en.wikipedia.org/wiki/Shaheen_Bagh_protests Accessed 15 Feb 2020.

[12] Swati Narayanan, https://www.ideasforindia.in/topics/social-identity/sex-ratios-and-religion-in-india-and-south-asia.html. Accessed 25 Feb. 2020.

[13] Swati Narayanan, Op. cit.

[14] Rakshinda Perveen, "South Asian Women in Politics," https://dailytimes.com.pk/166437/south-asian-women-politics. Accessed 20 Feb 2020.

[15] Chapa Perera, https://www.lk.undp.org/content/srilanka/en/home/Blog/2015/12/11/Sri-Lankan-Women-in-Politics.html. Accessed 15 Feb 2020

[16] Chapa Perera Op. cit.

[17] Flavia Agnes. "Redefining the agenda of the Women's Movement within the secular framework," in *Women and the Right-wing Movements: Indian Experiences*, ed. Tanika Sarkar and Urvashi Butalia, London: Zed Books, 1995, 138-57.

[18] Ellen Turner, reflecting on the above article by Flavia Agnes, "Empowering Women, Feminist Responses to Hindutva, Intersections," in *Gender and Sexuality in Asia and the Pacific* Issue 28, March 2012 http://intersections.anu.edu.au/issue28/turner.htm.

[19] Flavia Agnes. "Redefining the agenda" 1995.

[20] Urvashi Butalia, "Community, state and gender: on women's agency during Partition," *Economic & Political Weekly*, vol. 28. No. 17, 1993. p.13.

[21] Serene Jones. *Feminist Theory and Christian Theology: Cartographies of Grace* (Minneapolis: Fortress Press, 2000), 29.

[22] Radhika Coomaraswamy. "Preface," in *'Honour' Crimes, Paradigms and Violence Against Women*, eds. Lynn Welchman and Sara Hossain, (London: Oxford University Press, 2007). xiii.

[23] Donaldson Laura E., *Decolonizing Feminisms: Race, Gender and Empire Building*, (Chapel Hill and London: The University of North Carolina Press, 1992) 7. See also Gabriele Dietrich who writes: "It has been an uphill task

to convince male dominated Dalit movements that sexual violence also has to be tackled if it is **not** inflicted by upper castes. In many instances, there has been an attempt to subsume women's concerns under the caste question, in a similar fashion as Marxists have traditionally subsumed questions of patriarchy under the class question." (In *Beyond Patriarchy, Caste and Capitalism* op cit. 13.)

Chapter 2

The Church as a Bastion of Patriarchy

We are Challenged to Review the Situation of Women in the Churches

After reviewing the societal context in this region, it is important to look at our churches and the status and role of women there. In churches in South Asia, the centralisation of institutional and ecclesial power seems to have become stronger over the years rather than contributing to the exploration of and living out a new community that is more adaptive to the communitarian spirit of our societies. The centralised missionary authority that existed in the time of the formation of the churches by mission boards have merely been taken over by Asian ecclesial heads (bishops and the ordained) and church councils that wield unjustifiable power over the resources of the church—finances, educational institutions, hospitals and human resources too. Women, except for a handful, find it hard to penetrate into these fortresses of power. We do have a few churches, from particularly the Orthodox family, that have more indigenous roots and trace their roots to the time of the Apostle Thomas. Regretfully, they too have imbibed patriarchal power relations from local cultures and from their origins.

The Intentional Domestication of Christian Women

Women in South Asia are systematically domesticated by the church. They are deeply influenced by an understanding of Christian anthropology (as described in the conclusion of the previous chapter). It is an understanding that "posits what could be termed *perpetual hierarchy* as God's will and intention for gender relations"[1]—and this has legitimised the inner doubts that women carry about themselves and their humanity. Christianity has tended to assert that the term "mankind" is inclusive of the experiences of women and men and embraces all that makes for what is human. This assumption of course works in many ways and "to a certain extent it becomes self-fulfilling in that women themselves begin to understand themselves through the male lens and in so many respects begin to see themselves as defective, insufficient or as simply experientially deluded."[2]

It is **the sin of complicity in self-destruction** that inhibits Christian women when they step out into the world. Mary Daly, the famed feminist theologian, has described women's "original sin" as their internalisation of blame and guilt.[3] The side effects of the internalisation of submissiveness by women, of being "the other," leads to a psychological paralysis—a general feeling of hopelessness and anxiety; of a false humility because they are taught that women should not rival men or threaten men's egos. This finally leads to emotional dependency and lack of courage. Eradicating this in the church would be basically redemptive for the whole community, as sexist oppression is dehumanising to both women and men—from the confines of the church it follows women into the world.

Violence Against Women—Even in the Church!

The biblical affirmation "made in God's image" has been the core theological message giving women the courage to face up to the challenge of dealing with the many forms of violence they experience and to recognise themselves not as victims but as survivors. Feminist theologians have asserted that since women are made in the image of God, women ought to resist all forms of violence against their bodies which epitomise the Body of God. Any form of violence against women is a form of aggression against the Body of God. Yet, in spite of this foundational Christian teaching, even Christian women in churches have been forced to acquiesce to abuse and the worst forms of violence. Women's bodies have been the site of possession, conquest and control because of dominant patriarchal cultures as also the values the church has promoted. In the recent past, nuns in India have begun exposing the psychological impact they have silently borne—some of them having faced sexual violence for years. A shocking example of this is of a bishop of the Catholic Church in India being accused by a nun from his diocesan order of having raped her on and off for four years. As a woman who has given her life to the church, she bore the humiliation silently, unable to speak out and tolerating the many times she was beckoned to his room and was abused by him. The court continues its deliberations, but the church has stayed firm in its refusal to take her word on what the bishop did to her and has protected him. She, on the other hand, has met with approbation and punishment. Sadly, other religious women are divided in their opinion, some saying the nun should not have spoken out against a bishop.

Marie Fortune,[4] who was one of the first to speak out against clergy misconduct, writes:

> It is unethical for a minister (clergy or lay) to engage in sexual contact or sexualised behaviour with a congregant, client, employee, student, etc. (adult, teen or child) within the pastoral, professional relationship. Crossing the sexual boundary is a violation of the pastoral role, a misuse of power and authority of the role, a violation of the vulnerability of the congregant, client, etc. and **lacks authentic consent (due to the other's vulnerability in the relationship.)**[5]

So powerful are ecclesial and societal pressures on nuns that they have come to believe that it is their fault and that they needed to put up to what they were experiencing. They had internalised the humiliation to such an extent that they would say that they were inferior beings who did not have the courage to recognise that they need not have been silent about the abuse. Many women in South Asia in the church and society are too ashamed and afraid to speak out.

To a feeling of inadequacy, one can add **the feeling of shame**. Women are made to feel a sense of shame about their bodies and their abilities. This adds to the diminished self-esteem and increases feelings of inferiority, incompetence and weakness. Authentic self-realisation is impossible when one is not aware of one's potentials (and limitations too). The shame of being female is projected in the body language of women—many young women assume a crouch rather than walk with their heads held high with pride in their God-given sexuality and the beauty of their bodies!

Additionally, there is the shame that is attributed to women because of their bodily functions of menstruation and childbirth. These normal processes have become one of the ways in which women are made to feel unclean and inadequate. Even today there are many women who do not partake in the Holy Communion when menstruating—some would even stay away from the church! By and large the concept of a woman staying away from the church for the initial 40 days after childbirth as she is considered unclean, and then being "cleansed" on the day she returns to the church, is no longer the required norm in many churches. But it is regretfully carried out implicitly in many places and is euphemistically called a blessing for a safe childbirth. Levitical law (Lev. 11-15, 20) that treats women as unclean and defiling of men restricts the full participation of many women in the public sphere even now. Bleeding symbolised death for a woman in biblical times because it identified her as taboo in her society—this is observed till date. in subtle ways, restricting the participation of women.[6] The skewed understanding of women's sexuality and their bodily functions as polluted and polluting has unfortunately been one of the key issues on deciding whether women should be ordained into priestly orders (in those denominations where it is being debated). (As an aside I would add that for Dalit women this is exacerbated further; we have heard of separate church buildings for Dalits and upper caste Christians in some places. The understanding that Dalit women will pollute their worship experience is strong among some upper caste Christian women of a particular denomination in south India!)

Sunday after Sunday one can observe in middle-class congregations how women impose on themselves restrictions in the way they dress, move and demonstrate reverence. They veil themselves even in churches where it is no longer required. Even in those ministries where they are "allowed leadership", they offer it with hesitance, taking a secondary position, and are afraid to play a role that could be perceived as them taking over power from the largely male clergy, church leadership and even from the men in their families, when they are present.

There is also the **concept of self-sacrifice.** Sacrifice, humility and reverence are not in themselves negative values—following Christ demands this of us—and they are also not necessarily gender-specific. However, it is a fact that in the church women are taught to make needless sacrifices to negate themselves and surrender their opportunities and interests in favour of the men in their families. Sacrifice must have a value for the one who makes it.... However, Christian women are taught from early childhood to sacrifice only for the other, surrendering their own interests and desires. "The concept of sacrifice has been construed in terms of self-negation... the general idea being that one gives up something good or of higher value for the common good."[7]

These are some of the ways in which the church has played a pivotal role in restricting Christian women's full participation in the life of the church and by extension in the public sphere. Feminist theologians have written extensively on each of these forms of domestication and control.

Some churches, such as the Church of South India (CSI), do ordain women (since 1984), and most dioceses of the Church have ordained women. Rt. Rev. Victor Premsagar, a former Bishop of the Church, described the situation in this way, "It is said that some dioceses have ordained women as deacons, **with the undertaking that they will not press for presbytery ordination.** Even when women are ordained as presbyters, they are not given the same charge and emoluments as the men presbyters."[8] Apart from a few brilliant exceptions, most women as ordained priests emulate their male peers or turn to the men and even their husbands for leadership or to get approval. Bishop Premsagar wrote this over two decades ago; unfortunately the situation remains unchanged till date. In the CSI's 70 odd years of existence, only one woman has been consecrated bishop.

Many Protestant traditions in South Asia have not yet ordained women even though there is an increase in the number of women who are responding to the call and appealing to their churches to sponsor them for theological education. Many women enter theological schools as independent candidates with absolutely no guarantee of a job. Women have to often give a written undertaking to their bishops that they will not come back and seek ordination or even employment in the church after they complete their theological studies. When ecumenical formation courses are offered by international ecumenical bodies, the churches predominantly send men who are mostly clergy for such training.

Ordained ministry is not the only way women serve the church or the community in Christ. All other ministries of the church—evangelism, Christian education, Sunday school, hostels, or social work ministries—have been undervalued, and workers in these ministries are underpaid. These are often the only openings for theologically trained women. While sustaining the struggle for ordination to priesthood, I believe that in this process we as women need to contribute to a redefining, refining and reconstructing of what priesthood is all about. Tokenism is a disease in South Asian churches; women are often included in committees, church delegations and so on to fill a required quota. Women in male-dominated environs are often pressured to operate by male rules and emulate male models, and they find it virtually impossible to go beyond male models or to offer a new kind of leadership— this includes ordained ministry.

Women's Organisations and Movements in the Church

While this is a major theme in itself, a brief mention of the role of the missionary movement in the lives of Asian women is necessary. Several examples of the impact of the missionaries on the "liberation" of Indian women can be mentioned: from education of women, the building of the "zenana" health mission for women, training women to be evangelists and catechists, to organising women for social reform.[9] Many mission boards headed by women began operating in the world and much of the property that mission agencies owned by the churches were funded with contributions from women in their home countries. The missiologist Dana L. Roberts writes: "Evangelical women saw themselves as helping to save the world through self-sacrifice and service. Their interest in spreading evangelical ideals throughout the world increased as the century progressed, so by the end of the century, 57 per cent of the subscribers to the London City Mission were women, 56 per cent of legacies left to the Baptist Missionary Society were from women and 70 per cent of all receipts to foreign missions were given by women and children."[10]

An important contribution of the missionary movement to women in the churches in the region was the organisation of women's work in the churches. All the major Protestant denominations (as well as Catholic and Orthodox churches) have strong women's auxiliaries/Mothers' Unions/Women's Fellowship groups and Orders of sisters that were formed almost at the same time the church was formed. These have in most cases been the only avenue open to women for leadership. Women's organisations have made an important contribution to the life of the churches by providing leadership training, Bible study and a considerable amount of fund-raising activities. However, it is unfortunate that very capable women are often lost to the church, busy as they are in their own little "women's fellowship" corner. The leadership of these organisations also gets entrenched in the hands of a few, and too often they administer these organisations in the same "patriarchal" and authoritarian pattern of the church. Some churches still have bishops as the leaders of these organisations so as to keep a check on how far the women will go! Women workers in these organisations are sometimes paid low wages and while volunteerism has been a key contribution of the churches to ministry, women who depend on these jobs for the survival of their families or to supplement the income of a family are in fact being exploited by the church.

Women in Theological Colleges

This was a gradual process. While the first batch of Bachelor in Theology students graduated in 1915, women entered the portals of theological colleges as students only in the 1970s. As the decades progressed, more and more women entered theological courses; in some colleges there are nearly 50 per cent women students. There have been reports of sexual abuse in some theological colleges; this is because there is an unfortunate divide between theological education and the daily lives of women. The theological college itself should provide an emancipatory environment for women where students would respect one another and where valuing differences and promoting each other's academic excellence would become the norm. Theological institutions should be built on the principles of democracy and shared power. Additionally, can just any woman or man teach women's studies or guide a student through an assignment to highlight the perspectives of women? Should not the female and male faculty have necessary credentials to teach a feminist approach to a subject? Are theological schools prepared for this? This gains credence when we recognise that women and men who go through theological training are then thrown into the life of a very patriarchal church and society. They need the resources to sustain a feminist approach to the questions that confront them in pastoral life.

Churches sponsor women to theological studies even if some of them are unable to assure them ordination to priesthood or jobs that relate to their theological training. Monica Jyotsna Melanchthon, one of the brightest feminist theologians today, delivering the Bishop and Mrs. Parmar lectures entitled Feminist Theologizing: Rethinking Theological Education in India at Leonard Theological College, in Jabalpur, Madhya Pradesh, India, a few years ago does have these words of caution about women in theological education:

> The relatively recent admission of women to an academic environment that is still dominated by male scholars and masculine values; the identification of both women and religion with characteristics that militate against the dominant intellectual paradigm of secular and even theological scientific rationalism, such as intuition, spirituality, emotion, relationality, and the poetics of language that expresses these dimensions of life; (and) the double marginalization of the woman scholar of theology or religion, because she must struggle against both the historical legacy of a sexual cultural ideology that continues to denigrate and devalue women in subtle but destructive ways and theological intolerance that is often hostile to women's scholarship and the presence of women in religious and theological studies departments in the academy.[11]

Perhaps the impact of the presence of women scholars and students in theological schools will take some time before it is recognised as a valuable resource for the churches in South Asia.

Emergent Theological Voices of Women Theologians

As mentioned earlier, in the 1970s and 1980s the women's movement found new strength and organisation and was engaged in critically analysing and exposing the patriarchal ideology existent in society and the ways in which the family and religions in South Asia legitimised and justified the violence that women experience. This gave the impulse for church women to become critical of the institutional church and its indifference to the violence that women experience in church and society. The church refused to speak out on issues such as the institution of dowry and the pressure it brought on poor families (as a matter of fact, the church was/is by its silence legitimising this outlawed practice, as it continues to solemnise marriages where dowry is given and taken). The church has also been silent about rape, domestic violence, abortion of female foetuses, etc. The women's movement in society motivated church women to reflect on violence against women and children in the life of the church itself. This provoked a discussion among the women in the church, who realised that the church was not an innocent bystander. The church has upheld patriarchy and has contributed to the marginalisation of women and to the trivialisation of women's spiritual and theological gifts.

At the outset, the movement of women in the church was also largely middle-class dominated. Therefore, the questions that absorbed women in the churches related to the ordination of women to priesthood, the use of language that excludes women in worship, symbols and rituals of the church that left out the experience of women, and practices that discriminated against women in the church. Additionally, violence against women in society, in families (even Christian families) and in the church did preoccupy church women. This led to a recognition that the inherited theology of the church as an offshoot of the church's colonial past was a hurdle. What made it even more complicated and difficult is that even the work of male liberation theologians (including Dalit and Adivasi theologians) did not attempt to analyse the oppression of women as systemic and as rooted in a larger structural economic, political, cultural and religious malaise in the country.

It was only after this initial period that **theology from the perspective of women** was first spoken of in different parts of Asia, including South Asia. It was a very tentative beginning but an important new impulse for women. In 1984, the women's unit of the National Council of Churches in India, called the All India Council of Christian Women (women of all the major Protestant churches and the Orthodox churches in India were part of this), the Association of Theologically Trained Women in India along with Catholic women, organised a national consultation titled "Towards a Theology of Humanhood: women's perspectives"[12] to begin this exploration. This was organised largely thanks to the impulse and encouragement received from the Women's Commission of the Asian Ecumenical Association of Third World Theologians. So tentative were the steps taken at that time that the women could not speak of feminist theology—it was titled "a theology of humanhood"! But this opened the way for the strengthening of a new movement of women theologising. This wave of change spread across Asia, including all of the South Asian region. Similar efforts were made in Pakistan and Sri Lanka.

We recognised that the Bible and our faith heritage have embedded within them liberation potential for women. Biblical texts, especially those relating to strong women in the Bible, and the message of inclusion, justice and love that is discovered in this text, inspired Christian women. Women began to declare boldly that the violence we experience in our everyday lives and the forms of discrimination we experience in the church do not have to be our lot. Women theologians, and also women in the pews, in women's fellowship groups and in association meetings, began reading the Bible anew and discovered a surprising new message of hope there. Jesus and his attitudes to women were central to this liberation story. This was a truly important moment for church women in India, because until then, most women did not believe it was proper or their right to reread the Bible or to interpret the texts. The domestication of women by the church had made them believe that it was the clergy (and therefore by and large men) who had the power to do this. Additionally, in those times women studying theology were few and far between.

Several examples can be given from India to show how the Bible and its stories came alive in response to the experiences of Indian women. One would be that which relates to the struggle we were engaging in at that time, regarding inheritance rights for Christian women. Archaic personal laws that governed Christian families (some of which still exist!) restricted our privileges as Christian women and gave us an unequal share of rights in the family, including the right to ancestral property. It was at that time that the story of the daughters of Zelophehad found in Numbers 27:1-7 made new sense. Women such as Mary Roy became to us like the daughters of Zelophehad when she courageously moved the Supreme Court of India as to why her ancestral property was denied to her. This ultimately led to a change of the law! The daughters of Zelophehad are right, we as women discovered through a rereading of this text!

There was the incident of a prominent film producer claiming on national TV in India that he "would hack his wife to pieces" if she was unfaithful to him! And suddenly, the concubine in the book of Judges 18 became very relevant to women's experience—to us as women this "text of terror"[13] brought home the senseless violence South Asian women live with. Women who often face the threat of being killed or of being "terrorised" at home in the hands of the family for not bringing in adequate dowry or simply because they are women can be treated in this way, as the first section of this chapter delineates.

Then, there are in the Bible stories of resistance and courage where women have played a leading role. Esther, Ruth, Abigail come to mind—all women who took matters into their own hands for the sake of their people. There are also the many encounters that Jesus has with women where he affirms them, names them, heals them, chastises the men around them and welcomes the women into his community. Simple stories such as the incident of Jesus healing the bent-over woman, as recorded in the Gospel of Luke 13, gave women a sense of hope that they do have a friend in Jesus, a religious leader who would not hesitate to even break the laws so as to ensure that women can stand upright!

The primary exegetical tool was women's experience of suffering and discrimination and their determination to resist. Women described this as anchoring themselves in the "vast ocean" of their experiences so as to "probe its depth." Stella Faria calls on women with these words, "Through our collective consciousness let us re-read God's word, with a new heart, and a new sense of identity with the word. Through this new perspective will emerge a fresh understanding that will enable and empower us to recreate or evolve biblical hermeneutics from women's perspective. Simply put, women need to refresh the Word and restore it to God's original and inclusive message which will not only liberate our souls, but will bring all women and men to wholeness."[14]

Towards the Church as Event… Steps to be Taken
Introduction: Given this context and story of women, what are the prospects reaffirming Church as Event? Do South Asian churches and women have a chance to liberate themselves? Is there hope that feminist theology will be able to have an impact on the churches and to lead them to transformative action? What ingredients does feminist theology need to become a force to reckon with? From the perspective of women, here are some ingredients that the church needs to work on to transform the role and potential for Church as Event in South Asia.

a.   A South Asian Feminist Epistemology

Reclaiming South Asian feminist epistemologies is the first task. The multilayered experiences of women, the stories of women in the history of our nations, as well as in myths, traditions and proverbs need to inform the truth and influence how the Bible and our faith can help us find answers to our struggles as women. In Christian feminist thought, the value of searching for a new epistemology has gained special significance. This is primarily rooted in the life experiences of subaltern women who "have privileged access to survival expertise."[15] They have embedded in them a "cunning" ability to survive in spite of the onslaughts of poverty and violence. Additionally, poor women are also the holders of knowledge systems as they are the ones who have lived in prudent relationship with the earth. It is they who (along with the men of their communities) have tried to resist projects of "development" that threaten to destroy the delicate ecosystems as well as their own livelihoods.

Monica Melanchthon reminds us that, "Whole arenas of our past as Christian women remain entirely unexamined, and there is scarcely a question on which there is not important work left to do. Our rich and complex cultures offer many different narratives to women (and to men), as tools for understanding others and ourselves. For centuries now the Christian woman has been and is still being controlled and influenced by the theology and ideology of the master narratives of the Bible and the Culture which support a power structure in which gender, class, race/ethnicity/caste, sexuality and ability all define who matters and how."[16]

An alternative feminist epistemology is based on a commitment to transform hierarchical structures of power and injustice so as to uncover the liberation potential of Christianity. The transformation of unjust structures is critical because traditional understandings of society emerge out of and are framed by centres of abusive power. Feminist epistemology is based on a desire to seek alternatives that are based on an ethic of care, compassion and mutuality in relationships. The question to be asked is whether these are "merely new topics to be reflected on and integrated into our traditional ways of thinking, or will dealing with them lead us to work at modifying the very models we use to think about the world?"[17] Traditional ways of knowing have been both androcentric and anthropocentric and therefore limited in their scope. What we need is a new epistemology, i.e., "to construct new styles of knowing that are intimately related to our new cosmologies."[18]

The task of reading the Bible together will challenge the assumption that any universalist constructions can be claimed uncritically. It is imperative that we as feminist theologians from all parts of South Asia, caste groups, ethnic backgrounds, regions and ages recognise that it is such claims that have legitimised the denial of the dignity and the value of diversity. It is this that has been at the heart of the neoliberal paradigm and of a monoculture and has legitimated the colonising and neocolonial/globalisation project of our countries as a whole but more particularly Adivasi and Dalit lands and the lives of the rural poor. Perhaps what is the most challenging for all of us is to recognise that none of us hold the final truth—but in a common quest we can move towards that.

While the tentative steps we took in the 1970s and 1980s are important, we were still dependent, almost entirely, on Western feminist theologians to discover how we can read the Bible anew. While we have to be grateful to feminist theologians from the West for their wisdom that liberated our reading of the Bible, I believe it also steered us into a particular methodology and scholarship that kept many Indian women out of the discussion—strengthening the divide between theologically trained women and women in the pews. It also did not open the space for us to reflect on the deep divisions among us as women—to have given the space for Dalit women and Adivasi women to voice their struggles as well as hopes for a new world right then. This would have strengthened the voice of women in the Asian church and society.

Additionally, our links with women theologians from other Third World contexts were limited. While the Ecumenical Association of Third World Theologians (EATWOT) network did provide some openings, these were not strong enough and only a few of us had access to these links anyway. Linking with Dalit and Indigenous women in India and with Third World feminist theologians from other Third World countries from those early times would have helped us to make our theological work more contextual, grounded, as well as more relevant and effective.

b. A New Feminist Methodology

Because of the work of women theologians, with the support and accompaniment of some male theologians, several theological colleges have started courses in Women's Studies/Gender Studies. This is a success story at the end of a long-drawn-out struggle. Additionally, several theological institutions have also added a paper to each branch of study focusing on women's perspectives on the topic—be it the history of Christianity, pastoral theology, or in Old or New Testament studies. This, too, is an important new initiative. However, changes in the theological curriculum cannot be enough if no attempt is made to transform the methodology of teaching and learning. To begin with, what is needed is a feminist pedagogy that will root theological education in the everyday lives of women. Only then will the struggles of women for identity, justice and dignity, in theological schools, in the church and in society be successful. As mentioned earlier, theological institutions themselves need to be revamped and prepared for teaching feminist theology and ethics.

Speaking of a new "womanist methodology" that roots itself in community, Evangeline Anderson Rajkumar writes: "The term womanist is borrowed from our African-American sisters who found in the word 'Womanist', coined by Alice Walker, an affirmation of themselves, a power to question their oppressors who were within their own territory. I have borrowed this radically political term from them to point out to the presence of similar challenges faced because of casteism and sexism. I would like to redefine the term 'Womanist' in the Indian context as that double consciousness which emerges to renounce casteism and sexism as inherently evil to humanity, and stands in solidarity and spirit for justice and equality, regardless. Womanist spirituality is a collective spirituality, one that is rooted in community."[19]

"We are the text," the Korean feminist theologian Chung Hyun Kyung reminds us—we embody in our lives, our sexuality and our struggles for life, the Asian woman's text of liberation and justice. Therefore, feminist theological pedagogy has to engage with "secular" women's movements and other movements working for social transformation in India and elsewhere. Feminist pedagogy has to lead us to what Monica Melanchthon stresses—not on the individual actions of women but on their collective actions when wrongs have to be set right. Citing the case of Judith and her servant in the Old Testament, Monica Melanchthon lifts up "the solidarity between the two women across generational, religious, class and ethnic affiliation"[20] as a model for women today and concludes with what we can learn and gain from this. "They were not only of different castes but different religions and classes, and a rewriting of these stories stressing the camaraderie between these women would perhaps provoke conversation between women of different caste communities to work for reconciliation between castes and the betterment of the society."[21]

c. With Women of all Faiths

A South Asian feminist theology has to open itself to dialogue with women of other faiths. We have to be constantly aware that all our faith traditions have inbuilt in them patriarchal biases and have, in one way or the other, been used to legitimise violence against women. Our religious traditions have been at the heart of patriarchy, leading to discrimination and exclusion, such as the abhorrent caste system. We also see again and again the way religious sentiments are used by vested interests to create a culture of fear and violence. Therefore, it is time for some honest and mutually critical dialogue among us as women of all faiths. We have, regretfully, boxed ourselves into exclusive ghettos and view women of other religions with suspicion and even distrust. At a recent meeting of feminist theologians, the inevitable discussion of Muslim women in *burkhas* (the veil) came up for discussion. The Christian women present saw it as a symbol of religious oppression. However, as Christian women we have never entered into dialogue with Muslim women and tried to understand why there is an increasing veiling of women in our world. Why, even in my congregation in the city of Chennai, a CSI congregation in a big city, I see an increase in the number of women covering their heads when receiving Holy Communion! A dialogue among us as women of all faiths will unravel what is happening in our society and why new rules of "protection" and "humility" are growing in a globalised world where difference is neither understood nor respected.

At the same time such a critical dialogical journey with women of other faiths will provide us the creative space to discover the liberation potential of all religions. We have to release our religions from their colonial bondage and make them relevant, effective and responsive to the Asia of today. This will also require us to read the Bible with new eyes. Musa Dube, the feminist theologian from Botswana, offers us a way forward. She says that we ought to "always insist on new spaces for cultivating new contextual and international readings-writings, which are both decolonising and depatriarchalizing."[22] This will draw us into a new feminist circle of "hybridity and inter-textual readings."[23] I would add here that such a reading would include the depth of wisdom and knowledge found not just in other religious texts but also from the oral religious and spiritual traditions—in the lives of women.

d. South Asian Feminist Theology ought to be Postcolonial: Affirming Hybridity, Relationality and Community as its Basis

Postcolonial does not refer to a period in history as colonialism continues to exist in some form or the other in all nations in South Asia. Neocolonialism, in the form of globalisation and other systems of domination, thrive. However, postcolonial theory offers a space for the once colonised to resurrect "the marginal, the indigene, the subaltern.... It is an act of reclamation, redemption and reaffirmation against the past colonial and current neo-colonising tendencies which continue to exert influence even after territorial and political independence has been accomplished. It is a tactic, a practice and a process. It means finding ways of operating under a set of arduous and difficult conditions which jeopardize and dehumanise people."[24]

What has interested me most in this theory which had its origins in the writings of thinkers such as Homi Bhabha, Gayatri Spivak and Edward Said is the emphasis it places on ***mutual interdependence, relationality and transformation.*** It describes the possibility for the construction of a hybrid identity not just between us as women of former colonised nations and our sisters in the West, but among us as women in South Asia, with all that threatens to divide us. It aims to overcome essentialisms and dichotomies. A postcolonial reading of our faith calls for an in-between-space. It offers the churches the possibility to reclaim the Bible and our faith as our own and to discover the qualities required to ensure that the church in South Asia is truly a South Asian church.

The liberation paradigm in most former colonies has emphasised that women must put themselves in a secondary role for the sake of the liberation of their peoples, either from colonial powers or from other forms of political, economic or social structures of domination. Women continue to be the poorest of the poor and are bowed down by all that is described in the first chapter of this book. Women have by and large been socialised, even by the church, to put their families and communities above their own personal interests. Sacrifice and humility as personal spiritual choices are indeed noble and deeply Christian virtues, but when it is imposed on the woman because she is female, it makes it a form of coercion and violence. This needs to be addressed.

e.   Reflections on Masculinity

It is a sign of hope that men are increasingly recognising the potential of their delving into questions of masculinity. Such an exercise is rooted in the Asian psyche but it has been suppressed by colonialism and the power of patriarchy aided and abetted by the caste system. The sociologist Revathi Krishnaswamy points out that the medieval Bhakti movement had made androgyny a powerful spiritual ideal.[25] In one stream of Hinduism, Ardhanarishvara is an androgynous deity composed of Shiva and his consort Shakti, representing the synthesis of masculine and feminine energies. The Ardhanari form also illustrates how the female principle of god, Shakti, is inseparable from the male principle of god, Shiva. Ardhanari in iconography is depicted as half-male and half-female, split down the middle. Therefore, the resources for the exploration of the power of masculinity in the liberation project are there before us. Such an exercise will empower both men and women to find the more caring, nurturing "effeminate" side[26] of their personalities and will contribute to a violence-free and just world for women, men and children. It will also contribute to a deconstruction of myths surrounding the caste-ridden Indian society.

The church has domesticated women as it represents what prevails in society. It is really not possible to speak of Christian women as one category of women since we are formed not just by our Christian identity but by our caste, class, language, region and education and denomination. Here we focus only on women in the pews. There is a commonality here that cuts across all castes, languages and all countries in this region as well as all Christian denominations—we are all formed by the same Christian teachings and practices that condition our participation in the public sphere. The situation of women in general and the increasing voices of hope in resistance movements, starting with Dalit women and moving to the kind of protests described above, impel us to review the status of women in the church. The majority of Christian women in the pews of the church are carefully hidden from the public sphere. The domestication of women in the church in South Asia has been pretty systematic and they have been, by and large, relegated to what can be termed as "housewifely tasks" even within the church. The ministries of caring, visiting the sick, of education of children and of beautifying the church for worship often falls on women. Their service and spiritual resources are used to the full in the day-to-day life of the congregations but they are basically confined to what they are told is the "security of the church" as a structure. (Unfortunately, we have discovered that even the church is not a completely secure place for women and children.) There is a particular Christian denomination in south India that has decreed that its women not be permitted to participate in night sessions in one of its major annual church revival campaigns, indicating a "protective" attitude to women which in a way stifles their participation. There are many ways in which the full and creative participation of women in the church and all its ministries are curbed.

There are, of course, many Christian women who are active in the political life of the countries of South Asia or are scholars in universities. There are Christian women politicians, writers, poets and thinkers, scientists and activists in social movements such as fisherfolk struggles, Dalit liberation movement, movements to protect the environment and the livelihoods of the poor. Christian women are active in every field of life, but they do this as citizens of the country and not because they are Christians. They do not necessarily need to declare their Christian identity in their public presence, except when it is politically expedient (largely to men who use this for their benefit). In keeping with the Christian heritage in this region, the education of Christian women in every field of study has brought them into the public sphere in a way. But in spite of this focused attention on the education of women starting with the missionary movement, we need to ask ourselves just how liberated Christian women are from the shackles of traditions and practices buttressed by patriarchy and caste. Can we imagine something new?

Endnotes

[1] Kristene E. Kvam. "Theological Anthropology," in *Dictionary of Feminist Theologies*, Ed. Letty M. Russell and J. Shannon Clarkson, (Westminster John Knox Press, Louisville, Kentucky, 1996) 11

[2] Marcella Althaus-Reid and Lisa Isherwood. *Controversies in Feminist Theology*, (SCM Press, London, 2007), 18

[3] Mary Daly. *Beyond God the Father: Towards a Policy of Women's Liberation* (Beacon Press, Boston, 1973), 49

[4] Rev. Dr. Marie M. Fortune is a renowned author, lecturer, ethicist, theologian, and a pioneer in the movement to end domestic and sexual violence. She is the founder of the Center for the Prevention of Sexual and Domestic Violence, now known as Faith Trust Institute in Seattle, Washington.

[5] Marie M. Fortune. "Pastoral Misconduct," in *Dictionary of Feminist Theologies*, 204.

[6] Hisako Kinukawa. "Purity-Impurity," *Dictionary of Feminist Theologies*, 232

[7] Elizabeth Amoah. "Sacrifice/Self Negation", *Dictionary of Feminist Theologies*, 254

[8] P. Victor Premsagar. "Women's Ordination: A Church of South India Experience," in *Women in Church and Society—Essays in Honour of Florence Robinson*. ed. Prasanna Kumari, (Chennai: Gurukul Lutheran Theological College and Research Institute, 1999). 138. Emphasis added.

[9] One such example is referred to the "Breast Cloth or Upper cloth movement", when in the mid-19th century, the missionary movement in the former Travancore State—now part of Tamil Nadu, India—supported the Chanar women in their struggle to cover their breasts. Till then this had been a privilege of the upper caste Nair women only. For more information on this and on other ways in which the London Missionary Society worked for the liberation of women, see Joy Gnanadason, *A Forgotten History: The*

Story of the Missionary Movement and the Liberation of the People in South Travancore (Chennai: Gurukul Lutheran Theological College and Research Institute, 1994).

[10] Dana L. Roberts, quoting F.K. Proshaka (Women and Philanthropy in 19th Century England, Oxford: Clarendon Press) in *The 'Christian Home' as a Cornerstone of Anglo-American Missionary Thought and Practice, Converting Colonialism: Visions and Realities in Mission History, 1706-1914* ed. Dana L. Roberts (Michigan/Cambridge: William B. Eerdmans Publishing Company, 2008), 138

[11] Monica Jyotsna Melanchthon, in one of the three Bishop and Mrs. Parmar lectures she presented on "Feminist Theologizing: Rethinking Theological Education in India" at Leonard Theological College, in Jabalpur, in January 2010. https://www.thefreelibrary.com/Doing+Asian+women%27s+theology.-a0365688936. Accessed 20 Feb 2020

[12] Aruna Gnanadason ed. *Towards a Theology of Humanhood: Women's Perspectives,* (Delhi: ISPCK, 1986)

[13] Phyllis Trible, *Texts of Terror,* this path-breaking book in which the author rereads four texts from a literary-feminist perspective—a new way to allow the text to "have its own way", as the foreword to the book describes it. She titled the chapters related to Hagar, Tamar, the unnamed concubine and Jephthah as "texts of terror" because of the horrific stories of violence they embody. *Texts of Terror: Literary-Feminist Readings of Biblical Narratives,* (Philadelphia: Fortress Press, 1984).

[14] Stella Faria. *Feminist Biblical Hermeneutics.* This was a keynote address at a seminar organised on the occasion of the Silver Jubilee of the Ordination of Women in the Church of South India, *Feminist Biblical Hermeneutics,* eds. Lalrinawmi Ralte and Evangeline Anderson-Rajkumar (Delhi/Bangalore IWIT/ISPCK, 2002.)28

[15] Vandana Shiva. *Staying Alive: Women, Ecology, Survival in India* (New Delhi: Kali for Women, 1988) 24.

[16] Monica Melanchthon. in the Bishop Parmar and Mrs. Parmar Lecture, 2010. Quoting Mary Romero & Abigail J. Stewart, (Eds.), *Women's Untold Stories: Breaking Silence, Talking Back, Voicing Complexity,* (New York: Routledge, 1999), xiii. Slightly adapted.

[17] Ivone Gebara. *Longing for Running Water: Ecofeminism and Liberation* (Minneapolis: Fortress Press, 1999) 21.

[18] Ivonne Gebara, 1999, 22

[19] Evangeline Anderson Rajkumar. "Turning Bodies Inside Out, Contours of a Womanist Theology," in *Dalit Theology in the Twenty First Century*, 201

[20] Monica Melanchthon. *The Servant in the Book of Judith*, 1999, 246

[21] Monica Melanchthon. 1999, 246

[22] Musa Dube. *Postcolonial Feminist Interpretation of the Bible* (St. Louis, Missouri: Chalice Press 2000), 119

[23] Musa Dube, 2000, 116

[24] R.S. Sugirtharajah. *The Bible and the Third World: Precolonial, Colonial and Postcolonial Encounters*. (Cambridge University Press, UK, 2001), 250

[25] Revathi Krishnaswamy. "Effeminism: The Economy of Colonial Desire," in *The Masculinity Studies Reader*, ed. Rachel Adams and David Savran, (MA, USA: Blackwell Publishing, 2002) 295.

[26] I am intentionally using this much beleaguered term—a full exploration of which has been done by Revathi Krishnaswamy in the book cited above. ibid.

Chapter 3

Celebrating Sexuality:
Redeeming our Bodies

An issue that requires focused attention is "human sexuality" because much of the violence women experience stems from their sexuality; and much of the discrimination they face is also because of their sexuality. A conversation on women and sexuality does not come easily in South Asia. Faith communities, including Christians, find it difficult to speak of the body and its senses. This is because, at the core of our religious practices is theological dualism that keeps in separate compartments our bodies and our souls—and all that is base is associated with the body. It is this mind-body dualism that characterises much of Christian thought and it is the lens through which both the Bible and church traditions have been interpreted, thus placing limits on people's experience of their sexuality, and which also has been instrumental in promoting the systematic suppression of sensuousness and sexual pleasure.

Sexuality is often seen as the antithesis of spirituality and is thus shunned. As a Lutheran World Federation handbook describes it: "…there is the mistaken tendency to think of the body as bad and the spirit as good…our bodies are to be considered good not inferior. Our bodies are 'God's temple' (I Cor. 3:16). They are sources of joy and delight, even if vulnerable to sickness, suffering, abuse and death. In the Apostle's Creed, we profess our faith in the resurrection of the body. This leads us to the central question as to how do we take care of our bodies as an aspect of an ethic of embodied care?"[1]

The feminist theologian Lisa Isherwood reminds us that Christianity is rooted in an incarnational theology and "it is necessary that a religion that throbs with incarnational redemption should at last release its followers from the prison of their own skins that the tradition has made. It seems that incarnational theology speaks of a world that experiences *metanoia*, as turning around through the skin."[2] Jesus came to us in human flesh to embody that promise. In such a context, Isherwood's question is pertinent, "How then is it that we have imagined that disembodied spiritual perfection is the way to make of this earth a heaven, the incarnate dwelling-place of the divine?"[3] She continues: "After all, the man Jesus, while being declared divine was also portrayed as a very earthly man—a man who made strong political statements through the powerful symbolism of touch and feeding."[4] Regrettably, the flesh which was once so important in "the finding and living of the divine has been swamped by the Word and made silent or is now seen as rebellious."[5]

Feminist Voices... Breaking the Silence

It was women in the churches who first broke the silence and engaged in affirmations of sexuality, which incidentally also opened the way for discussions on homosexuality. This happened because in a context where female bodies have been the target of abuse and violence, women have realised that they have to reclaim their bodies and celebrate their sexuality. Sexuality had to be retrieved out of the grip of patriarchy that has ensured that the family and the state and market forces stay in firm control through rigid definitions of sexuality and through the appropriation of women's bodies and their reproductive rights.[6] Violence and the subjugation of the body have been given theological justification in institutionalised forms of religions and their teachings which have marginalised and domesticated the female and the feminine, thus shackling women and even legitimising violence against them.

The docile, subservient image of South Asian women ensures that they dare not celebrate their sexuality or stake claim to their bodies. Such a mindset persists in the family, in the church and in society. What is needed is an alternative theological paradigm drawn out of the lived experiences of women in the struggle to keep their bodies in their own control. It should become a subject of discussion in our theological discourse if the church is to provide a word of assurance to South Asian women. If the church would continue to profess that women, like men, are made in the image of God, then the affirmation of the sexuality of both women and men is imperative.

Lisa Isherwood, in her beautifully articulated theology of sexuality, writes, "Theology must celebrate the body and religious practice should become more embodied and sensual—sensuous sacramentality becoming the order of the day, a riot of smell, colour and most importantly, touch. A celebration of all our senses and a connection with the organic sensuality of the earth and each other. We need to be awakened and this is unlikely to happen with a piece of dry wafer and warnings about the sins of the flesh. Incarnation demands more engagement."[7]

This becomes an urgent challenge for the churches in this region because at present dealing with human sexuality has been largely relegated to the entertainment industry and media, to the scientific community, to powerful patriarchal forces in the family and in the social structure of Asian society such as the caste hierarchy with its underlying principles of pollution and purity associated with the body. The distorted attitudes to human sexuality have given rise to multifarious cultural practices of discrimination and even violence against women, children, sexual minorities and other oppressed groups such as Dalits.

Compulsory heterosexuality is demanded in a context where women's fertility is controlled within a patriarchal system that places a glorified emphasis on motherhood.

The family, along with the state today, has sought to control women through rigid definitions of sexuality and appropriate for itself reproductive rights and control over a woman's body. Violence and subjugation have been woven into institutionalised forms of religion whose patriarchal tenets have marginalised and domesticated the female and the feminine, shackling her and legitimising violence against her. Social and legal codes of justice have either been blind to crimes against women such as wife battering and prostitution that have in fact received tacit social approval, or have seen violations like sexual assault and rape as acts of individual aberration and deviance and has even rendered some totally invisible, as in the case of homophobia.[8]

Unwritten family codes force a good many to hide their homosexual identity or to express it only surreptitiously. They dutifully get married, as is demanded of them due to social pressure, and act out their parts as husband or wife—dropping their mask only when they are amidst people of their own sexual preference. They are expected to project a veneer of being "normal"—what happens outside of the public eye is ignored. Some churches, as for instance several churches in India, under the leadership of the National Council of Churches in India (NCCI) have recognised the need for a pastoral response from the church.

Asir Ebenezer, General Secretary of the NCCI, describes it this way:

> NCCI started this journey as early as 2001, when we had the First Study Institute on Human Sexuality, when church leaders came together at an ecumenical level and engaged with the LGBTIQA+ communities for the first time…. We recognise here, with much humility, that this process of sharing the struggles and joys in a community with confidence and openness has continued over all these years. There is now a synergy between those marginalised and the visible Church in the form of you and me empowered by the presence and discerning guidance of the Spirit of God.[9]

As part of that journey in December 2009, the NCCI, along with the Christian Institute for the Study of Religion and Society, the Student Christian Movement in India, and SCEPTRE, a programme of the Serampore Senate of Theological Colleges, organised a meeting of theologians, church leaders, pastors, and others. The conclusions of that meeting were put together in a statement that affirms:

> …sexuality is a divine gift, and hence God intends us to celebrate this divine gift in committed, consensual, and monogamous relationships. It is in such celebrations of our sexuality that we grow into the fullness of our humanity, and experience God in a special way. We believe that our negative attitudes towards sexuality and our body-denying spirituality stem from our distorted understanding of God's purpose for us. The embodied God who embraced flesh in Jesus Christ is the ground for us to love our bodies and to celebrate life and sexuality without abuse and misuse. God invites us to experience sexual fulfilment in our committed relationships of justice—love with the commitment to be vulnerable, compassionate, and responsible. We recognize that there are people with different sexual orientations. The very faith affirmation that the whole human community is created in the image of God irrespective of our sexual orientations makes it imperative on us to reject systemic and personal attitudes of homophobia and discrimination against sexual minorities.[10]

The NCCI has followed through this programme through ESHA (which used to be called the Ecumenical Solidarity for HIV and AIDS) and National Ecumenical Forum on Sexualities and Gender Diversities, which has brought out a "Policy on HIV and AIDS: A Guide to the Church in India" that was passed in the NCCI's General Assembly in Shillong in 2008 with the focus on Human Sexuality and Gender Diversities.

The Bible and its Ambivalence: Finding Redemption in the Text

The Bible is explicit in underlining that God created us male and female and placed us on the earth with specific sexual roles and responsibilities. Both the Old and the New Testaments directly address sexuality issues and send messages that are quite different from what we have too often been taught by the churches and our denominations. Texts related to sexuality in the Bible give us sexuality education: many Bible stories and many of the laws in the Bible contain information to help people understand the important role that sexuality plays in our lives. What we do understand through some of the texts that refer to sexuality is how the people who wrote down the Scriptures understood sexuality in their own times. By understanding that the Bible is contextual to another period, we can, in the process, gain insight into the Bible's ability to speak to us today on these moral issues—in a changed world with a new understanding of sexuality and of sexual relationships.

As feminists have repeatedly pointed out, there are "texts of terror"[11] in the Bible where women are the objects of male desire, of violence, and are pawns in the hands of men and thus subject to sexual abuse and resulting in the use and abuse of sexuality by women themselves in pursuit of political ends. While we are quick to quote from the Bible texts which seemingly condemn homosexuality we often gloss over and even condone the many instances of how the body is used in the story of the Jewish people. We read about the sexual games played by Ruth; of Lot's daughters; of Abraham and Isaac who pass off their wives as their sisters in clear violation of biblical law; of Sarah who was taken into Pharaoh's palace, implying that it was for sexual relations with the Pharaoh, and of Abraham who is complicit in this. We read of Jacob marrying two sisters, Leah and Rachel (also illegal according to Levitican law), and of the sexual transgressions that underlie David's lineage. Intrigue, lust and murder surround the stories of Abigail and Bathsheba with David. These are but some examples, but somehow we accept them as the history of the survival of the nation of Israel, and in fact acknowledge this as part of Jesus' lineage! These stories become "covertly positive in the political fate of ancient Israel: God, it would seem straddles both sides of the legal fence in order to advance the fortunes of his chosen people."[12] We need to talk about this and why the church and its members gloss over these examples of the use of sexuality which render women as either silent partners in the crimes or as victims of the political, economic and social designs of men.

But then we are quick to condemn texts that refer to homosexuality (e.g., Gen.9:21-27; 19:4-11; Lev. 18:22; 20:13: Deut. 22:5: Judg. 19: 16-26; I Kings 14:24; 15:12; 22:46). Many of these texts in fact condemn sodomy—they are not referring to homosexual love which is often confused with instances of sexual abuse in the Bible. And even if in the Bible some of these texts point to the sinfulness of human behaviour, they are placed in the context of unequal power relations and to the abuse of power and are therefore one-sided in both their articulation and in interpretation. Carol S. Robb writes: "Definitional perspectives on sexuality in Christian theology are linked to different proposals about *control of sexuality.*

In Hebrew Scriptures, sexuality is a source of defilement to be controlled with purity laws, and it is a source of (male) gratification and of heirs to be controlled by property laws. For early church writers and Reformation theologians, sexuality is a source of passion that tends towards chaos unless it is controlled within the family, for the purpose of procreation and where children can be cared for."[13]

Feminist biblical scholars such as Monica Melanchthon urge us to go a step further, as the texts of terror mentioned above tend to reinforce negative stereotypes about sexuality and in fact legitimise the silencing of women's sexuality. What feminists like her have done is to take some of these "difficult" texts from the Bible and deconstruct their meanings and reconstruct the exegesis of the texts so as to restore to them their redemptive value. As women move away from a position of victimisation to find strength in their survival roles, such new reinterpretation is truly liberative. One such text Monica Melanchthon has worked on is found in Genesis 19:1-38—the story of Lot and of the destruction of Sodom, mentioned above. This is a text often used to legitimise the condemnation of homosexuality. She reads the text from a liberation perspective to show how the daughters of Lot in fact take control of their sexuality and ensure the future of their people. Lot fades from the story and the two daughters take centre stage to save the family lineage. She writes, "Genesis 19 provides the reader with the opportunity to reflect on the issues of human sexuality and the problems and injustices that are perpetuated by certain constructions of sexuality."[14] By giving agency to the daughters of Lot, she is redeeming them from the "victim" role attributed to them (even by feminist theologians) to become the liberators of their people. In like manner, one could read the role Queen Esther plays in the liberation of her people or the role Ruth plays with Boaz— both of whom use their sexuality to win a point!

Unfortunately, over the centuries, the church has not uncovered those texts that help us celebrate our bodies and our sexuality and teach us our role in respecting our own bodies and the bodies of others (for example, the Song of Songs). However, any attempt to unravel the meaning of the Bible has to be situated in the contemporary context and with the new tools developed to read the Bible so as to draw from the text moral wisdom for today in order to develop a revised sexual theology. Both Scripture and church history are far richer on sexual issues than most people assume and we need to draw on our heritage rather than get trapped in popular understandings of theology and sexual morality. We cannot depend on the media and what are considered socially acceptable forms of behaviour and of relationships as the norm for determining our attitudes to sexuality. Our faith in Jesus, who taught us how to accept all and live together as a community that puts aside all distinctions, ought to be what guides us and governs our lives.

The Missionary Movement and its Attitudes to Sexuality

The Protestant missionary movement of the nineteenth century brought to South Asia sexual values prevalent in England and other parts of Europe at that time. For example, in a study of the missionary movement and its impact on

Asian women, Mrinalini Sebastian quotes from the Basel Report of 1874 where notions regarding appearance and purity were part of the blueprint for another mode of living, a "more civilized mode," and they list sensuality as a vice along with other negative traits.

> We are happy to state that by far the greater part of our former pupils are attached to us, and they appreciate the benefits received from us during a number of years. Such young women make mostly good wives and mothers. Those who are the least thankful are generally untidy, and scarcely show the labour bestowed on them whilst they were in school. There are several girls in the institution, who fill our hearts with misgiving, when we think of their future. **Sensuality, stealing, lying, quarrelling, pride, loquacity, are vices which seem to form their second nature**. The greater part, however, cheer us through their obedience and good behaviour, and a few through their fear of God.[15]

The church in South Asia is caught in an awkward space between its biblical and theological mandate to play a pastoral and ethical role; the church's past history and formation; its patriarchal moorings; and the aggressive role that the capitalist free market plays, especially on the media and in the commercialisation of sex and sexuality. In addition to this we need to address the issue of attitudes to homosexuality as an important dimension in the church's responsibility.

In South Asia and other parts of Asia, there is evidence to show that AIDS spreads mostly through heterosexual relations—of men carrying the virus to their homes. In a patriarchal context where women have limited control over their own bodies and sexuality, it increases their vulnerability to HIV/AIDS. "Good" women are expected to be ignorant about sex and passive during sexual intercourse which makes it difficult for them to be informed about risk reduction or, even when informed, makes it difficult for them to be proactive in negotiating safe sex. The tradition of girls remaining virgins restricts their ability to ask for information as they will be thought to be sexually active if they make enquiries; the widely held belief that sex with a virgin would cleanse men of sexual diseases; economic insecurity that makes it acceptable for women to have unprotected sex for money; and sexual violence against women—all remain major barriers to HIV prevention and care. Reports of rape, incest, wife battering and desertion in the South Asian context point to the fact that sex is often coerced, and this is in itself a serious risk factor for HIV spread and infection.

South Asian churches need to focus on the rights of homosexual men and women. As said earlier, Christianity and the church have had great difficulties in dealing with homosexuality. Often Christians who know they are gay struggle within a homophobic environment. Their parents are unable to give them the support they need because they have themselves grown up in a church and religious environment where they have been taught that the Bible has branded homosexuality as an aberration, even a sin. The parents go to pastors or counsellors requesting their support to "heal" their children of this "disease", as they understand it! Unwritten family codes force most gay men and women in India to hide their homosexual identity or express it only surreptitiously. A large number of homosexual men and women are content to lead a double life. They dutifully get married, as is demanded of them due to social pressure, and act out their parts as husband or wife, dropping their mask only when they are amidst people of their own sexual preference. They are expected to project a veneer of being "normal"—what happens outside of the public eye is ignored. This, of course, poses serious mental and emotional pressure on gay and lesbian young people. In some cases, it ends in suicide in a society which prefers silence on this issue. Many churches have not yet become "Christ-like enough" to support a person who wishes to "come out" by giving him or her a way in which to cope with his or her sexual orientation, so as to be true to themselves.

Towards a New Sexual Theology for South Asia

This is the task before theologians and churches—to find a new language that will liberate the churches to stand in solidarity with sexual minorities and with those who suffer from HIV/AIDS, based on the gospel mandate to show compassion and love to all those who need the compassion and love of the church. But, at the same time, we need to turn to the gospel and our faith to learn how, with humility, we can recognise our sin of intolerance and our refusal to acknowledge that God created us in our wonderfully diverse sexualities. But, regretfully, by our selective reading of the Bible and our limited interpretations of the texts, we have continued to sustain the archaic mind/body dualisms that place restrictions on our potential to be a healing and accompanying church.

How can we set aside our prejudices, our predilections and our limitations and turn to the Word of God and find there the Jesus who refused all forms of discrimination and provided a welcome to all, especially the weakest in his society? As we know, he constantly interpreted the Scriptures to make them relevant and come alive to the community he was ministering to. We now have the ethical and moral responsibility to do the same—to live as a Jesus community of acceptance, love and respect.

Endnotes

[1] *Grace, Care and Justice, A Handbook for HIV and AIDS Work*, Department of Theology and Studies, LWF, Geneva. 2007.

[2] Lisa Isherwood. *The Good News of the Bible, Sexual Theology and Feminism,* (Sheffield: Sheffield Academic Press, 2000). 13.

[3] Lisa Isherwood. *The Good News of the Bible,* 2000, 13.

[4] Lisa Isherwood. *The Good News of the Bible,* 2000, 13.

[5] Lisa Isherwood. *The Good News of the Bible,* 2000, 14.

[6] As early as 1993, Asian women made this statement in a gathering affirming their concern over the violence against lesbian women in Asia. The gathering that was held in Bali, Indonesia, was called by the World Council of Churches with the Christian Conference of Asia and the Asian Women's Human Rights Commission. The Bali Declaration, Asia, August 1993, is published in *Together with Courage: Women and Men Living Without Violence Against Women*, WCC, Geneva, 1998.

[7] Lisa Isherwood, 2000, 32.

[8] The Bali Declaration of the Asian Regional Consultation on Violence Against Women, held in Bali, Indonesia, organised by the World Council of Churches, the Christian Conference of Asia and the Asian Women's Human Rights Commission, 1-6 August 1993. (Emphasis added).

[9] Asir Ebenezer, "Preface," in *Building Inclusive Churches: Engaging with Human Sexualities and Gender Identities. A Training Manual for Churches,* (ESHA Programme of CSA/NCCI and Kerk in Actie, 2019).

[10] Statement of a meeting of theologians, church leaders, pastors and others organised by the National Council of Churches in India with the Christian

Institute for the Study of Religion and Society, SCEPTRE, a programme of the Serampore Senate of Theological Colleges, and the Student Christian Movement in December 2009.

[11] Phyllis Trible. *Texts of Terror. Literary-Feminist Readings of Biblical Narratives.* (Fortress Press, Philadelphia, 1984).

[12] David Biale. *Sexual Subversions in the Bible, Sexuality (A Reader)*, eds. Karen Lebacqz and David Sinacore-Gunn (The Pilgrim Press: Cleveland, Ohio) 1999. 382.

[13] Carol S. Robb, "Sexuality," in *The Dictionary of Feminist Theologies*, Eds. Letty M. Russell, J. Shannon Clarkson, (Louisville, Kentucky: Westminster John Knox Press, 1996, pp. 257-258.

[14] Monica Jyotsna Melanchthon. "Bible Study on Sexuality Genesis 19:1-38" in *Created in God's Image, from Hegemony to Partnership*, eds. Patricia Sheerattan-Bisnauth and Philip Vinod Peacock. (Geneva: WCRC/WCC Publication, 2010) pp.161-169.

[15] Mrinalini Sebastian. "Native Bible Women and the Missionary Ideal: Reading the Archives from a Post-colonial Feminist Perspective," in *Journal of Feminist Studies in Religion*, Volume 19, No.1, Madison, NJ, USA.

Chapter 4

Women:
Nurturing the Earth, Protecting Life

For us, the rivers, the forests, and our land

are the basis of our existence,

This earth is our mother.

No one can snatch her away from us.

No one has the right

to take away our land from us.

We therefore take an oath today

that we will always protect

our land and rivers.

Large dams being built in this area

are drowning our forests,

our mountains and our land.

We pledge never to let this happen.

A solemn pledge by the people in a mass gathering against the Subarnarekha dam project.[1]

South Asian nations are walking swiftly on the competitive road to become "developed" nations—this is the ideology, the ambition that drives every policy, every political programme in these countries. The onslaughts on the earth and on the life of the poor of the earth challenge the flourishing of life and a sustainable future. The powers that be focus on the desires and needs of the middle and upper classes so as to persuade them into believing that this so-called "development" is what will give them a better life. All this in a bid to ensure that they who rule are voted back to power, even if they are corrupt and however anti-poor and short-sighted and lopsided their policies may be. For example, the demand is for faster and faster internet connectivity (even if it means destroying small publicly owned networks and lining the pockets of big business houses in India), while millions still live with little or no electricity—the list goes on. Denuding forests, destroying green stretches, digging into mountains and the earth, polluting the waters at an absolutely unsustainable pace, and eroding the life, livelihood and dignity of millions of people, particularly the poor, seems to be the only way to ensure the "development" of the nation for the benefit of a privileged minority. The life of millions of the poor seems to have no value at all!

Women have been Protesting Against the Setting Up of a Nuclear Power Plant

In June 2016, *The Guardian* newspaper carried a report that said: "Women are leading protests in Tamil Nadu state in India against a nuclear power plant—yet few people in India know the village they're from, let alone support their cause. Their campaign, since the late 1980s when they were first proposed, had been against nuclear reactors coming up near their villages; it became more vehement since 2011 when the first reactor was fuelled. Celine, 73, was among the protestors, who take it in turns to go without food. 'Not a single government, not a single political party is willing to take up our cause,' she says. 'Only Mother Mary can save us now.'"[2]

The Guardian writes a moving testament to the women and their courage in this protest. "As India 'develops', its energy needs are growing rapidly. More than 300 million Indians are still without electricity.... India consumes a whopping 872m tonnes of oil equivalent for power; only China and the US use more. Its annual energy import bill is 120 billion dollars, which will grow to one trillion dollars by 2040.... The Indian government presents nuclear energy as part of its 'clean energy' solution to its looming energy crisis. The Nuclear Power Corporation of India was set up, according to its mission statement, to 'produce nuclear power as a safe, environmentally benign and economically viable source of electrical energy to meet the increasing electricity needs of the country.'"[3] However, the women have become aware of the impact that disasters in faulty reactors and leaks can cause to people. They knew about the 1986 Chernobyl disaster, and the fact that these reactors in Koodankulam against which they were protesting were Russian left them with little comfort.

Despite billions of dollars of investment in nuclear power, the figures from the Department of Atomic Energy in India (DAE), obtained by *the Guardian*, suggested that nuclear plants produced 37,456m units of electricity, which covered just about 2 per cent of the country's annual consumption needs. Anyway, the electricity produced would be used by industrial establishments and not for domestic use, people fear. *The Guardian* report said many countries had taken a slice of India's budding nuclear energy market: the United Kingdom, Canada, the United States, Australia and Japan had all offered expertise and resources.

Nuclear plants, backed by foreign governments, are dotted around all South Asian countries…some are being built. Yet foreign governments have shirked responsibility for the impact these units will have on the people living in the locations where they are set up. When US President Barack Obama visited this region a few years ago, he signed a deal limiting the US' legal liability in the event of an accident at a nuclear plant.[4] The women know just how dangerous this could be to the environment and to their lives and just how vulnerable they were and what relief they would get in case of an accident. Their struggle here did not end well as the reactor has continued to operate.

These are among the examples of the many women-led movements in different parts of India demanding closure of so-called "development projects" that are in fact death-dealing to people. Now the latest news is that a 5-km radius around the Koodankulam plant is out of limits to the people who live in surrounding villages and towns, fuelling further suspicions of the safety of the reactor.

Nalaka Gunawardene from Sri Lanka writes on the "Critical Nuclear Issues in South Asia" in the *Asian Scientist Magazine*:

> South Asian countries are stepping up using and collaborating in civilian nuclear technologies. In pursuit of new opportunities, however, it is imperative that governments address safety concerns adequately. Greater public understanding is also needed so that people can distinguish between nuclear weapons, nuclear energy generation and other nuclear applications in various spheres of development. Right now, conflation is common which, in turn, causes confusion. Nuclear matters have long been contentious in India and Pakistan due to government secrecy surrounding military applications. Both countries possess home-built nuclear weapons, but neither has signed the Treaty on the Non-Proliferation of Nuclear Weapons which came into force in 1970. Specifics of their arsenals thus remain unknown.[5]

Later in the same article, he writes,

> Nuclear energy activities are somewhat more open, though no less controversial. Both India and Pakistan have functional nuclear power plants which generate around four percent of electricity in each country. Opinion is divided on the cost-benefits of nuclear power. Environmental and radiation safety issues have come into sharp focus since Fukushima nuclear accident in Japan in 2011 and some new plants in South Asia have drawn sustained public protests. Eclipsed by these debates is the use of radioactive isotopes in agriculture, food preservation, water management, healthcare and industrial processes. Beneath media's radar, these have been going on for decades. Our challenge is to scale up these applications while increasing the entire sector's transparency and public accountability.[6]

An Ecofeminist Approach and Theology from a South Asian Christian Perspective

The history of the church in Asia shows examples of the negative role played by Christian missions to undermine the value attached to the earth and to its sacredness by Indigenous peoples. Colonialism and the desire to "develop" nations that had led to conquest and occupation and the extraction of resources/wealth of colonised nations was closely linked to a particular understanding of Christian theology. As such ideology persists even now, it is urgent that Christianity turns towards the earth and the people of the earth.

Ecofeminism recognises that the protection of the earth is closely linked to other systems of injustice and discrimination—the issue of intentionally instituted poverty and other forms of discrimination, including colonialism's and neocolonialism's role in the use and abuse of both women and the earth; social structures of injustice such as caste and ethnicity too have played a contributory role in denigrating women and the earth. Therefore, an ecofeminist vision is inspired by the knowledge of poor women, particularly Indigenous and Dalit women. They carry within their life experiences traditions of prudent care with which they have lived on earth for centuries. Many Indigenous communities of women try to recover patterns of spirituality that connect them to their roots and to their traditional wisdom—often having to work against forces that attempt to stifle their histories, their knowledge systems, their lands. For many of them destruction of the earth is destruction of life itself. Theirs is a different world view, a different epistemology, a different analysis, and they offer unique spiritual resources and they contribute to the care of the earth.

Indigenous women speak of the earth as mother in a relational sense. There is no space for romanticism here, as they too face violence in the domestic sphere, as mothers and as women. Therefore, one uses the motif of "motherhood" with caution because of the oppressive and dehumanising ways in which motherhood has been appropriated by patriarchy. However, when Narango Puri, a Gond (a Tribal* Group) woman in central India, referred to the selfless love that the earth as mother has for all her children, her language did not seem to have similar patriarchal overtones. Narango said matter-of-factly: "Earth is like our mother, like a mother who cares for her children selflessly. As humans we go through the life cycle—we give birth, we nurture our young ones at the breast, we grow and we die. The earth will never die, but this requires that we as women who go through the same processes of birthing and caring for our children need to also nurture the earth."[7] She was also quite pragmatic in her response as to why they considered some groves and mountains to be sacred. "The sacred groves are seed banks—and have a diversity of plants. Therefore, we worship them. We never touch this life source but allow regeneration there. In this way the sustainability of the earth is protected." Narango ended our conversation by saying, "We may die, we may face death, but we will not leave the land—we will not be separated from our mother."

What can we as South Asian feminists learn from Narango Puri and other Indigenous and Dalit women to reclaim and redefine the relational and "sacrificial" value of motherhood, debunking it of the expectation patriarchy has imposed on it? From the context of the political engagement of Adivasi women in Odisha and other parts of India, it is evident that motherhood is symbolic of political action for a healed earth—it cannot be reduced to a biological role as has been emphasised in patriarchal societies. It is this transformed image of motherhood that has inspired ecofeminist theological reflections on the image of the earth as the body of God and as the mothering womb of God.

Protestant Christianity and Its Ambivalence about the Earth

This discussion becomes important if we consider the ambivalence of Protestant Christianity in Asia and some of the mistakes made in Christianity's mission history which had in some instances dismissed the customs, practices and spiritualities of Indigenous peoples in derogatory ways and labelled them as "pagan and animistic." In recent times, Indigenous theologians have begun to interrogate this history and some elements of Christianity that subvert environmental goals. Wati Longchar, an Indigenous theologian from Nagaland in North East India, writes:

> Creation is the first act of God's revelation. God cannot be perceived without water, wind, trees, vegetation, sky, light, darkness, animals or humans. It is the first act of revelation. God revealed himself/herself as *co-creator* with the earth…. God is present in creation. The presence of God makes the earth sacred. That is why God entered into a covenantal relationship with all creatures…. The major problem in theology is the articulation by faith of human history without taking into consideration all the members of the earth's family.[8]

In the face of large-scale environmental damage, the urgency of this task cannot be underestimated. The question to be asked is whether feminist theologies and the theological gifts of Indigenous peoples, Dalits and other subaltern communities have had any impact on the Christian understanding of creation theology. The epistemologies of women and other groups on the edges of society can influence theological teaching and the churches in South Asia. Regretfully, this impact is minimal as Christianity is still immersed in inherited Christian theologies and has remained deeply entrenched in a Eurocentric missionary past and a patriarchal worldview.

Earth Care: Some Ethical Values that Ecofeminism Offers to Church as Event

Towards a new way of relating with each other and with creation: Christian faith, its theology and, more particularly, feminist theology do contain the potential to provide a liberation ethic that would challenge all forms of oppression—between human beings and between humanity and the earth. For example, Letty Russell underlines that feminist theology "reaches for a new mode of relationship: neither a hierarchical model that diminishes the potential of the 'other' nor an 'equality' defined by a ruling norm drawn from the dominant group, but rather a mutuality that allows us to affirm different ways of being."[9] To ecofeminists the critique of anthropocentrism is related to the refusal of humanity to recognise the patriarchal fundamentals of the destructive way we live on earth. It is a critique of systems and structures which has privileged the male and not just all men but those who plunder the earth for profit and fail to recognise the integrity of the earth and all life forms, including the lives of those communities that live on the earth and nurture it. In this context it is important to acknowledge the work of ecotheologians such as George Zachariah, who would stress the importance of a form of anthropocentrism so as to reclaim the agency of people's movements in resisting development projects that destroy ecosystems. He calls this a "non-anthropocentric anthropology that affirms the being and becoming of a new humanity in the community of creation."[10] Therefore, when feminists in India would reject androcentrism (males as norms of humanity) they have to take this a step further and be bold in rejecting all forms of domination and exclusive values between human beings and between human beings and the earth—anthropocentrism. Additionally, what is required is an epistemological shift that renders to the earth its integrity as well as explores ways in which we listen to the wisdom of the earth and all the children of the earth.

The ethic of ecojustice as the frame of analysis: Both the poor and the earth cry out for justice. Nature can be seen as the new poor, "not the poor that crowds out the human poor, but the 'also' poor; and as such it demands our attention and care."[11] This requires political engagement to transform the injustice that is done both to the earth and to the poor—it calls for a merging of political activism and a spirituality of resistance. It calls for our engagement as theologians with people's movements such as the ongoing struggles referred to above, because our participation in their struggles for liberation mediates our own liberation. In fact, it requires more than an intellectual reexamination of the way we have done theological ethics, it calls for "a new discipleship journey—a detour in the way we live our faith."[12] In exploring with Indigenous women the depth of their ecological wisdom, we can learn a new ethic of care. This is not to legitimise the language of biological determinism that presumes some kind of inherent link between women and nature. But as Narango Puri said: "There is a radical relationship between the woman and the land"—to her it is about the relational character of humanity with the land. Women emphasise the interdependent character of the radical relationship[13] between the earth and humanity and the urgency of an ethic of care that women can offer to the earth in its distress.

Reclaiming women's ways of knowing—feminist epistemologies: For ecofeminist theologians, therefore, an alternative epistemology is based on a commitment to transform hierarchical structures of power and injustice so as to rediscover the liberation potential of Christianity. This implies social action to question and resist unjust structures and systems of knowledge that are framed by centres of abusive power. Ecofeminist theologians call for an overcoming of dualistic and hierarchical ways of knowing and bringing to centre stage the wisdom and knowledge of subaltern communities. This is based on an understanding that in such knowledge we will find resources to reverse the ecological destruction that has been caused by dominant ways of knowing and so-called scientific forms of inquiry. This also demands new ethical judgments on what is good, just and sustainable.

Vandana Shiva articulates this well:

> The intellectual heritage of ecological survival lies with those who
> are experts in survival. They have the knowledge and experience
> to extricate us from the ecological cul-de-sac that the western
> masculinist mind has maneuvered us into. And while Third
> World women have privileged access to survival expertise, their
> knowledge is inclusive, not exclusive. The ecological categories
> with which they think and act can become the categories of
> liberation for all, for men as well as for women, for the west
> as well as for the non-west, for the human as well as the non-
> human elements of the earth.[14]

An Ecofeminist Vision in South Asia is Therefore an Eco-just Feminist Vision[15]

The crucial hyphenated word "eco-just" qualifies an South
Asian ecofeminist vision. Dominant ecological discourse has
not adequately addressed the interconnections between the
economic and ecological dimensions of life. Neither have
they affirmed the spirituality of hope and resistance that
lies in the wisdom of the people most affected by the earth's
distress. The solutions lie not just in individual actions of care
for the earth but in the transformation of an unjust world
order. There seems to be reluctance to relate with the political
dimension of the church and mission history with regard to
the conquest of nature and of the earth. These theologians
do not address questions of unequal power relations in our
world and the way this impacts the earth.

An Ecofeminist Vision Affirms More Compassionate Images of God

This calls for a new understanding and language for the
image of God. God, in India, from an ecofeminist liberation

perspective, is in fact shaped by Asian cosmology, which affirms the interdependence of all forms of life, the dialectical harmony between humanity and the divine; between human beings and the earth and between the male and female principles.[16]

God intervenes in a caring relationship not in a dominating way. But God is not reduced to the world because God transcends human understanding, therefore no one image would suffice.

The model of the world as God's body[17] encourages holistic attitudes of responsibility for the care of the earth and for the vulnerable and the oppressed; it is non-hierarchical. Both in God's immanence and transcendence, the image of God is found within us and in all of creation. Kwok Pui Lan, the Hong Kong/US theologian, writes,

> We can come to know God through nature as well as through human history. There is no separation between 'special revelation' known through the specific Christian story and the so-called 'general revelation' known through nature and wisdom from other cultures.[18]

An earth-friendly God is a God of compassion, who has "profound reverence toward life, empathy towards those who suffer and concern for the flourishing of all beings."[19] The focus of such an understanding of God is not on human beings alone but on all of life. Ecofeminist theologians draw on God's reciprocal relationship with the earth and with humanity—interconnecting the spirit and matter. God's spirit is accessible to us only in the body, i.e., the world. The world is not just nature, the good creation, but also society, the way human beings interact with one another and with nature. Whenever we inflict violence on the earth and on the vulnerable ones on the earth, exploitation and violence are done to the body of God.

Ecofeminist theologians therefore call for a shift from an implicitly dualistic, hierarchical, individualistic and utilitarian subject-object relationship with God and with the earth to a subject-subject relationship which values the integrity and goodness of all of creation. This will naturally draw us into understanding our image of God anew in terms of relationality. God as the resisting, struggling poor woman—of God as one who brooks no injustice and who protects the earth; of God as community—emphasising the inextricable link between the divine, humanity and all of earth. God as a mothering, nurturing woman is perhaps the most crucial for our times.

Many voices, many forms of wisdom are needed—among them the ecofeminist theological vision with its commitment to prudent care and transformational ethics is offered. Would the churches and the ecumenical movement recognise this as women's contributions to the present and the future of the earth and to Church as Event?

Endnotes

[1] People in a mass gathering against the Subarnarekha dam project in Jharkhand (former south Bihar), *Voices of the Adivasis/Indigenous Peoples of India*, ed. Sarini (Delhi, India: All India Co-ordinating Forum of the Adivasis/Indigenous Peoples, 2001), 65. Quoted by Aruna Gnanadason, *Listen to the Women: Listen to the Earth*, (Geneva: WCC Publications, 2005), 1.

[2] https://www.theguardian.com/global-development/2016/jun/06/lonely-struggle-india-anti-nuclear-protesters-tamil-nadu-kudankulam-idinthakarai 6, June 2016. Accessed 20 June 2018.

[3] indianpowersector.com/2010/09/npcil. Accessed on 11 November 2018

[4] https://www.theguardian.com/global-development/2016/jun/06/lonely-struggle-india-anti-nuclear-protesters-tamil-nadu-kudankulam-idinthakarai 6, June 2016. Accessed 20 June 2018.

[5] Nalaka Gunawardene, in "Asian Scientist" magazine https://www.asianscientist.com/2015/03/features/critical-nuclear-issues-south-asia/.

[6] Nalaka Gunawardene.

[7] Aruna Gnanadason, *Listen to the Women! Listen the Earth!* (Geneva: WCC Publications 2005) 99-102.

[*] The expressions Tribal, Adivasi or Indigenous Peoples are all used in this text as the communities of Indigenous Peoples use all these words to identify themselves.

[8] Wati Longchar. "Indigenous Theology in Asia" in *Asian Theology on the Way: Christianity, culture and context*, ed. Peniel Jesudason Rufus Rajkumar, (Lon,don: SPCK, 2012). 94.

[9] Letty M. Russell, *Feminist Interpretation of the Bible* (Philadelphia: The Westminster Press, 1985) 116.

[10] George Zachariah. *Alternatives Uncorporated: Earth Ethics from the Grassroots*, (London: Equinox, 2011) 123-124.

[11] Sallie McFague. *Super Natural Christians: How we should Love Nature* (Minneapolis: Fortress Press, 1997) 6.

[12] George Zachariah. *Alternatives Uncorporated,* 2011, 9.

[13] Sallie McFague. *Life Abundant: Rethinking Theology and Economy for a Planet in Peril* (Minneapolis: Fortress Press, 2000). 18. McFague explores the concept of the radical relationality reflective of the wisdom of Indigenous women such as Narango Puri in Odisha.

[14] Vandana Shiva. *Staying Alive: Women, Ecology and Survival in India,* (Delhi: Kali for Women, 1988) 224.

[15] This formed the main focus of my DMin Thesis submitted to the San Francisco Theological Seminary, DMin in Feminist Theologies. I adapted my thesis as a book and published by the World Council of Churches, Geneva. *Listen to the Women! Listen to the Earth.* 2005.

[16] Geraldine S. Smyth, A Way of Transformation: A Theological Evaluation of the Conciliar Process of Mutual Commitment, (Bern: Lang, 1995) 66.

[17] Aruna Gnanadason. "Toward a Feminist Eco-theology for India," *Women Healing Earth, Third World Women on Ecology, Feminism and Religion* (New York: Orbis Books,1996), 74-81.

[18] Kwok Pui Lan, *Introducing Asian Feminist Theology*, (Sheffield, England: Sheffield Academic Press, 2000) 75-76.

Chapter 5

Reimagining Church as Event!

... India is going through a very critical phase since its secular and democratic texture is under fire through the promulgation of the Citizenship (Amendment) Act, 2019 (CAA). The exclusion of Muslims in the CAA is the first instance of religion being used overtly as a criterion for citizenship and so, this gives expression to the 'divide and rule' strategy of a nationalistic government. This move risks tearing the country apart by destroying the basic tenets of the Indian Constitution **that declares India as a sovereign, socialist, secular and democratic republic.**

In this political climate that is divisive and discriminatory in nature, the Indian Christian Women's Movement wants to make a counter move that is unifying and inclusive. We want to affirm the bonding of all people as children of one God and citizens who have equal rights in this great country.

As a gesture that gives expression to this inclusive vision, ICWM members will conduct the foot-washing ritual this year, mainly with our Muslim sisters and brothers in our local units. This simple act of humble service can be a gesture of acceptance and above all a powerful declaration of inclusion and solidarity.

We draw inspiration for this event from Jesus Christ (John 13: 1-17), who in washing his disciple's feet, subverted the social hierarchies of his times and gave it a new meaning of inclusion and belongingness. When Peter as a disciple refused to allow Jesus, his master and Lord to wash his feet, Jesus was firm in stating "Unless I wash your feet, you can have no part with me" (Jn 13: 8) and he invited his followers to do likewise."[1]

"You are part of me!" was the title of the invitation sent out to the units of the Indian Christian Women's Movement encouraging them to link with the protesting Muslim women and offer them the solidarity of Christian women in their struggle against a law that could well disenfranchise many in their community. Christian women in India subverting the church to become the church—Church as Event! The proposed action as delineated above responds to the feminist theological compulsions outlined in the previous chapter and marks a radical shift from the church as a stultified institution to the church as event! A rereading of the text (John 13:1-17) and the adoption of this sacred symbol of Jesus washing the feet of his disciples—here of Christian women washing the feet of Muslim women—make the much-maligned and harassed Muslim women "a part of us." Muslim women, fully veiled, as propriety and modesty about their sexuality demands it, moving into the public space, with the men of their community stepping back and giving leadership to women—and for Christian women participating in an action of solidarity in that public space which transcends any Christian-Muslim dialogue we can have.

The Indian Christian Women's Movement was born five years ago.[2] Women of the Roman Catholic Church, Protestants from different denominations, and Orthodox churches came together to form a new movement of women who declare with one voice that as Christians we are restless for justice. As women we are able to cross boundaries that divide us by church affiliations to speak with one voice as Christian women in India. The ICWM has already sent an open letter to the Prime Minister of the country expressing women's deep anguish at the decision of the government to pass a law of citizenship that intentionally excludes the Muslim population from the definition of illegal immigrants who have lived in India without documentation. Added to this the law proclaims that only those who can provide documentation as proof have the right to citizenship even if they have lived here and contributed to the economic, political and cultural development of the nation for generations. In a country of gross poverty and inequalities in education and other means to development, it is estimated that several million Muslims will be rendered stateless within a few months.

Muslim women organised themselves against this law in an unprecedented way. For nearly two months they sat in silent protest in major cities (in some cities this is over 1,000 Muslim women in *burkhas*). ICWM units in Delhi, Mumbai, Bengaluru and Chennai visited the Muslim women as a sign of solidarity and empathy with them. This women-led "foot washing ceremony" was meant to be a way for Christian women to visibly demonstrate that we too, in remembrance of Jesus in these days of Lent, would "subvert social hierarchies" and give "new meaning to inclusion and belongingness."

The ICWM has also spoken out strongly against the rape of a nun by her bishop over a period of four years. Its statements of protest came after some members of the movement joined public demonstrations calling for legal action against the bishop and made strong demands to the

Church to strip him of his bishopric. The Church, however, through a carefully orchestrated campaign on behalf of the bishop, has repeatedly tried to silence the survivor nun and those in her order and others who have believed her narration of the incidents of rape and stood by her. Many, including the ICWM, have continuously supported her case for justice and provided her pastoral care and legal help.

While this sounds like an isolated case it does expose the deep malaise that inflicts our churches. The abuse of women in the church is one of the most carefully guarded secrets and one of the most gross of the sins committed by the church. In such a context it is our belief that such acts of protest and solidarity with the most marginalised is the only way we can strip the church of its efforts to silence women and to challenge it for its institutional and hierarchical forms of governance and pastoral ministry.

Such efforts become important when women, even in denominations that supposedly recognise the presence of women's theological, spiritual and pastoral gifts and do ordain them to priesthood, discriminate against them by not honouring their skills, rarely giving them independent charge of congregations, paying them less than the male clergy and, engaging in other forms of subtle and overt discrimination. Patriarchy governs the church, and women find little space to voice constructive criticism or offer alternative paradigms of service. Those who obey the rules of the hierarchy and do all they can to please those in power are able to flourish. Women in all our churches face this malaise.

But it has also given the impetus for some women to subvert the Church into becoming Event! When a woman pastor encourages the women of her congregation (without the permission of the bishop or anyone else) to make a detour on the way to a meeting organised by their bishop to join hands with women from many political parties and secular movements participating in a human chain on a main thoroughfare in Chennai in South India, is that not Church as Event? We were protesting the sexual abuse of women by local politicians in a town called Pollachi in Tamil Nadu, India, and as one of the women from her congregation described it, "Through the Lenten season we have been praying for these abused women—are our prayers enough? We felt the imperative to protest too!"

Some Crucial Voices in our Journey to Make Church an Event

Dalit Women's Voices

Without doubt the contributions of Dalit women to theology is another mark of Church as Event! A review of Dalit literature in the 1970s and 1980s reveals the almost near absence of Dalit feminist theologising even in male Dalit theological work. Thankfully, a handful of younger Dalit theologians today are trying to right this wrong. They are boldly reinterpreting history, myths and biblical texts from the experiences of Dalit women. As Prasuna Gnana Nelvala describes it, "Dalit women are those who have lost their laughter, labour, and life for the sake of upper caste men and women and even their co-Dalit men. Dalit women are completely neglected and ignored, dismantled, diminished, and distorted human beings."[3] She goes on to write: "Both the Dalit movement and the feminist movement share a common concern and discuss the issues of oppression and liberation. However, both failed in giving space to the experience of Dalit women, which is different and distinct from their Dalit male and caste female counterparts since their own oppression is a complex mingling of caste and gender debilitations."[4]

With this as the background, Evangeline Anderson-Rajkumar claims the title "womanist" to describe her Dalit feminist identity. To her, a womanist is "one who is conscious of the fact that individuals, man and woman, are social constructs who often internalize the patriarchal system as normal and ideal. A womanist is one who is willing to confess and repent of one's silent participation and consent to the system of caste and sexism anywhere. A womanist is one who is always looking out for ways of affirming human relationships in communities, and celebrates with joy the empowerment of the least, specially the Dalits and women who represent the most marginalized in the Indian context."[5]

What a privilege the church and the women's movement would miss if the creativity of Dalit women theologians did not influence theological transformation. These women have given new meaning and significance to myths, literature and historical incidents related to women as well as to the forgotten and ignored, lesser known women in the Bible. Monica Melanchthon reclaims the story of Bathsheba[6] from male theologians and from dominant feminist scholarship by reconstructing the character. According to Monica Melanchthon, focusing on "the victimhood of Bathsheba has in some ways blinded us from seeing possible strategies for survival and life after rape/sexual violation."[7] She also discovers the Song of Songs as a "metaphor for the new moment in the genealogy of Indian women."[8] There is also the "discovery" of Habra (by giving her a name) and reminding the reader about the silent, forgotten but brave maidservant in the Old Testament apocryphal book of Judith.[9] By doing this, she and other Dalit feminists are reconstructing Bible stories and stories from Indian mythology and history, all of which "often operate as 'master narratives' when they subsume many differences and contradictions, and restrict and contain people by supporting a power structure in which gender, class, caste and ethnicity all define who matters and how."[10]

Monica Melanchthon goes beyond this. She knows that Dalit women are too often portrayed either as submissive, broken characters or as heroes—both do not refer to the daily lives, hopes and aspirations of millions of Dalit women. She sees the task of Dalit feminists as giving these often-forgotten female characters "visibility, voice and agency" and by doing this contributing to the "identity and self-esteem of all marginalized."[11]

Adivasi Women and Ecofeminist Theologies

The last decade also witnessed an increasing number of Adivasi (Tribal/Indigenous women) entering theological schools—in fact, there are more women studying theology from the Adivasi belt of India than from other parts of the country in most of the theological schools in India. The search for recognised theological courses draws them to large institutions in the rest of India and their presence is inspiring as they bring new insights into theology, both from a cultural perspective but more importantly from an ecofeminist perspective.

Lalrinawmi Ralte, for instance, has made a significant contribution from her own Mizo background. "As I have studied Mizo history and folktales, I have seen that there is a tradition of women being given a very important place in the Mizo society and religious life. This happened even within the strongly patriarchal Mizo structure. Women were once considered the upholders of culture and religious life. Why this did not continue once Christianity was brought to Mizoram is an important question to ask." [12] In this article and in other places she explores how the present church in Mizoram and in the other North East states has used the Bible to legitimise patriarchal attitudes and practices, particularly in the church. Elsewhere she writes:

"Doing Tribal Women's Theology is sharing. Sharing is a reflection of all forms of life experiences of their suffering in every aspect. Sharing our silent suffering of bloodshed, starvation, dehumanization and the violations of human rights to the tribal people is empowering as much as frightening…. Again, doing tribal women's theology is struggle…. Women are the upholders of the church by various ways such as fund raisers, church goers, upholders of the broken churches and comforter of the hopeless members. If women are ordained, their contribution can be much more and the church will grow. Struggle is a rediscovery of the strengths of women both in the past and in today's life. By rediscovering their power, we affirm their contributions in order to make our life better. Still again, doing Tribal Women's Theology is commitment. This commitment is for the economic growth, for the protection of the ecological crisis, and the reconstruction of the disorder social systems that degrade women. Commitment for the liberation from various oppressive forces of economic, social unjust structures and religious inequality. Commitment for the service of God to uplift the less privilege people, to share their struggle, to lead them to the hope of Salvation to God. We share our cry to God, we struggle to reach God, we commit ourselves to liberate others. God is our only hope of liberation and everyone can be the agents of change for the betterment of the marginalized people."[13]

The reclaiming of those aspects of Adivasi culture that are liberative have led women such as Lalrinawmi Ralte, Narola Imchen, R.L. Hnuni, L.M. Narola, T. Vanlaltlani, Lalnghak Thuami and Limala Longkumer to name a few, to go into the Bible text in the context of their own lives.[14] Some of them explore what they have termed as "cultural hermeneutics"— that is an exploration of fables, myths and wisdom of their traditional cultures against the liberative message of the gospel. Additionally, the liberation message of the gospel has inspired them to challenge oppressive cultural practices in their societies, particularly in the church.

Without doubt the most important contribution of Adivasi theologians and resistance movements has been in the area of reflecting theologically in the area of ecology. Without romanticising the struggles of Indigenous peoples in India, it is important to acknowledge that Adivasi feminists challenge the Christian tradition and, more particularly, feminist theology for not just its androcentrism but for its anthropocentrism.

Given the facts mentioned above on the impact of ecological degradation on women in India, feminist theology needs to take serious note of the contributions of Adivasi theologians.

I believe that **ecofeminist theology** does contain the foundations for a liberatory ethic that would challenge all forms of oppression—for all of humanity and for the earth. Therefore, I have in my own work used "eco-justice" as the frame of analysis. Both the poor and the earth cry out for justice. Nature can be seen as the new poor. In the writings of ecofeminist theologians in India, for example, Ivy Singh, Gabriele Dietrich and I, we have called for the merging of political activism and a spirituality of resistance to transform the injustice that is done both to the earth and to the poor—and this has informed our theological work. Ivy Singh explores the ecotheological significance of the Narmada Bachao Andolan (Save the Narmada Movement) against big dams on the river that is not just destroying ecosystems but the lives of millions of Adivasi and Dalits who live along its course[15]. Gabriele Dietrich has explored the theological significance of the struggles of the fishing community in coastal Tamil Nadu and Kerala[16]. What Leonardo Boff says is fully relevant to Asia. He speaks of social ecology as the way that social and economic systems interact with the natural ecosystem, and "since the human race is part of the environment, social injustice goes hand-in-hand with ecological injustice."[17] As ecofeminist theologians we stress that our commitment to the earth and to peoples of the earth need be held together in one frame.

For Adivasi women, political engagement in the struggle against mining, the damming of rivers and other operations of the government, sometimes on land they consider sacred, is a natural corollary to the ethic of care.

"Traditional" ecotheology has not adequately addressed the interconnections between the economic and ecological dimensions of life. Neither has it affirmed the spirituality of hope and resistance that lie in the wisdom of the people most affected by the earth's distress. The solutions lie not just in individual actions of care for the earth (in recycled paper and bottles, for instance) but in the transformation of an unjust world order where consumption, greed and waste have become the norm.

Marks of Resistance: The Commitment to Survive

I began by speaking of the newly emerging voices of resistance. A small coterie of women in India from all religious traditions are saying "enough is enough" and are finding creative and constructive ways to survive and to challenge forces of exclusion and violence. Women seek new theological and spiritual resources for their faith journey. I would add that such signs of hope also lie in movements of men around the world who stand in solidarity with women.

The task before us to make Church as Event is twofold:

1. To affirm and work for a secular South Asia—this is not to give up our Christian identity or desist from pursuing a feminist liberation perspective of our faith. It is not just to tolerate women of other religious traditions; it is about working with women

of all faiths, especially with women of minority religious communities, to work for the dismantling of patriarchy in all religions and to work for economic, political and social justice for all in our countries. To follow Christ is to walk the road of secularism, and women are well-placed to demonstrate this. Such engagement will place us as Christian women in the public secular sphere.

2. But for this to be achieved it would require the reconstruction, contextualisation and updating of our theological explorations, liturgies, teachings, doctrines and structures to respond to the present context in South Asia today—particularly of women in the church. Feminist liberation theology and certainly Dalit feminist/womanist theology offer many challenging and new directions. The church and theological establishments can learn from feminist theologies and therefore need to include them in the curriculum. Ursula King writes: "Born out of the struggle to overcome the oppression and subordination of women, feminist theologies are linked to a powerful vision of equality, justice, liberation and hope, rooted in a faith that knows of redemptive transformation and wholeness of being. Doing such theology out of the perspective of praxis, the concrete socio-economic and personal histories of particular women in particular communities and churches means that it can only occur in contexts of radical plurality."

Now we would no longer speak of all women as being in one universal whole. We recognise and affirm the patriarchal systems of graded subjugation that divide our societies in general and that these exist within the community of women itself; therefore, to ensure that Christian women will engage in Church as Event requires a dismantling of systems of caste-ethnicity and patriarchy. This will free Christian women to engage with courage and conviction for justice and peace. Let us together walk and live the path of secularism.

Church as Event is about a celebrating community where all diversities are welcomed and honoured; all voices heard and yet with a focused advocacy for women, particularly subaltern and poor women. This is the vision of feminist liberation movements in the church and society. For women, Church as Event is a round table where children, people of all genders, Indigenous peoples and Dalits, people with disabilities, people of all faiths and no faith at all sit together in company with a healed and vibrant earth. Church as Event frees women to speak out, to dance in wild abandon, to celebrate the gift of their minds, their bodies, their hearts, their spirituality and their commitments to contribute to this alternative vision of the church where all will gather and act together to overcome all forms of injustice and to usher in a new world of justice and peace for all.

Endnotes

[1] In the communique sent out by the National Team of the ICWM to the regional/local units and other women as an invitation to reach out to Muslim women and organise this ceremonial act of "subversion" as Jesus did;

and of solidarity "with the least" as Jesus taught his followers. Regretfully the outbreak of the COVID pandemic interrupted these plans. But reaching out to Muslim women will continue on the agenda of the ICWM.

[2] The proposal for the formation of the Indian Christian Women's Movement (ICWM) emerged at the National Women's Conference on the theme "Paradigm Shifts in Vatican II and its Impact on Women" co-organised by Streevani Pune, NBCLC Bangalore, ISI Bangalore, Montfort Social Institute Hyderabad, and CBCI Office for Women at the NBCLC, Bangalore, from 8 to 11 January 2014. The presence of an ecumenical sister as a resource person, who voiced the need for a common body of Christian Women in India, helped to consolidate the decision to the birth of the ICWM.

[3] Prasuna Gnana Nelavala, "Caste Branding, Bleeding Body, Building Dalit Womanhood: Touchability of Jesus," *Dalit Theology in the Twenty first Century: Discordant Voices, Discerning Pathways*, Eds. Sathianathan Clarke, Deenabandhu Manchala and Philip Vinod Peacock. (New Delhi: Oxford University Press; Geneva: World Council of Churches. 2010). 267.

[4] Prasuna Gnana Nelvala. 267.

[5] Evangeline Anderson-Rajkumar. "Turning Bodies Inside Out: Contours of Womanist Theology," in *Dalit Theology in the Twenty first Century*, Ibid. 202.

[6] Monica Jyotsna Melanchthon. *Gender, Religion and Kultur,* Theologischen Akzente, Band 6 ed. Tenata Jost (Stuttgart: Kohlhammer Verlag, 2009). Forthcoming publication.

[7] Monica Melancthon. *Gender Religion and Kultur,* 2009.

[8] Monica Jyotsna Melanchthon. *Song of Songs,* 85.

[9] Monica Jyotsna Melanchthon. "The Servant in the Book of Judith: Interpreting her silence telling her Story," *Dalit Theology in the Twenty first Century,* 231-251.

[10] Monica Jyotsna Melanchthon. The Servant in the Book of Judith, 231.

[11] Monica Jyotsna Melancthon. 234.

[12] Lalrinawmi Ralte. "Cultural Hermeneutics,"*Feminist Hermeneutics,* ed. Lalrinawmi Ralte and Evangeline Anderson-Rajkumar (Delhi: ISPCK and IWIT. 2002) 92.

[13] Lalrinawmi Ralte. *In God's Image,* Vol. 19/4 2000.

[14] Regretfully, there are not enough published writings of Adivasi feminist theologians in English. They have contributed quite a bit in many books and journals, but there has been no compilation of these.

[15] Ivy Singh. *Voices from Narmada: Doing Ecofeminist Theology*, (Delhi: ISPCK, 2009).

[16] See for instance Gabriele Dietrich's article, "The Earth as the Body of God: Feminist Perspectives on Ecology and Social Justice" in *Women Healing Earth: Third World Women in Ecology, Feminism and Religion* (London: SCM Press, 1996).

[17] Leonardo Boff. *Ecology and Liberation: A New Paradigm* (Maryknoll, NY: Orbis Books, 2000), 88.

Ruth, Naomi and Orpah: A Story of Solidarity and Community

Text: The Book of Ruth

Supplementary Text: John 13:12-17, 31-35

Recently I reconnected with one of my Muslim friends; we did our BA Hons and MA in English Literature together at the university in the city of Bengaluru. She went on to do her doctoral studies in English Literature, got married and now lives in Karachi where she was a Professor at the university. We were very good friends when in college. I have been to her home and she to mine many times over, apart from going out together for movies and other activities. We stayed in touch with occasional contact. Now a common friend from college has brought a group of us together onto a WhatsApp chat group. This means we have been in touch almost every day for the past two years or so! We have shared information about our families, our work, our lives, our hopes and our dreams. The recent controversy about Kashmir and the Indian government's stance made the Indians in the group vociferous in rage but Qamar was silent… but then she broke the silence by making a passionate plea to us to oppose the dreadful atrocities being committed in Kashmir. Political comments are rare between us but she could not resist to comment this time!

I mentioned that it would be so good if we could visit her in Karachi. The Indians in the group were all excited, and started dreaming of the visit. But Qamar became quiet again! She knows it is not so easy for us to visit each other! On another occasion, the conversation was on the mangoes in another friend's garden in Bangalore. She invited us all to her home when they ripened. Then Qamar remarked with sadness in her tone that we are divided and kept apart by political and historical forces—we cannot just drop into each other's homes. I wonder when we as friends will ever be able to come together. We live in a world that divides us even if we are in solidarity with each other!

This introduction led me to choose for this Bible study the book of Ruth that centres mainly on the solidarity between three women—Ruth, Orpah and Naomi—intermeshed with the account of the relationship between nations and peoples. Elimelech and Naomi, along with their two sons Mahlon and Chilion, leave their own city of Bethlehem in Judah and migrate to the foreign land of Moab for the most obvious reason. They were seeking greener pastures because of a famine in Judah. We are aware of the number of people who have criss-crossed the globe to escape famines and economic and political hardship in search of greener pastures, starting with the great migrations from the European region to the

Americas and Africa to the present-day economic or political migrations (escaping persecution) across the globe. We also read that migrants who seek a home in Europe or North America have not been welcomed in.

To go back to the Bible story, the two sons of Naomi and Elimelech get married to Ruth and Orpah, two Moabite women. Unfortunately, all three men in the family die, leaving Naomi with her two daughters-in-law to make tough choices. Naomi decides to return to Judah as the period of famine has passed and there is evidence of plenty in Judah. As they prepare for their journey, Naomi tells her daughters-in-law to stay back and return to their own ancestral homes. Both refuse at the outset, but then Orpah does leave her mother-in-law and returns to her own home. Ruth, however, continues with Naomi to Bethlehem.

The Bible narrative has the potential to build Church as Event! It provides us the framework to relook at the way we have been taught to relate to each other. An important detail in this story is that the two daughters-in-law are Moabites. Moabites were not a welcomed community; they were considered to be traditional enemies and corrupters of Israel. Laura E. Donaldson, a Native American theologian, writes, "For centuries the Israelites had reviled this people as degenerate and in particular, regarded the Moabite women as agents of impurity and evil. Even the name 'Moab' exhibits this contempt, since it allegedly originates in the incestuous liaison between Lot and his daughters"[1] (Gen. 19). Ruth insists on staying with Naomi in spite of the poor opinion about her people. She refuses to leave, saying words that have become familiar, "Do not press me to leave you… where you go I will go, where you lodge, I will lodge, your people shall be my people and your God my God" (Ruth 1:16).[2]

Ruth eventually remarries Boaz, a wealthy relative of Naomi's husband Elimelech. According to the Malawian theologian Isabel Apawo Phiri, while in Ezra 10 and Nehemiah 13:23-27, God is presented as being opposed to Hebrew men marrying foreign women, "in the book of Ruth, God is seen as blessing a foreign woman, Ruth, and enabling her to conceive a child who became the grandfather of David, the king of Israel."[3] Laura Donaldson writes, "Rather than a rejection of the Moabites and acceptance of the Israelites…Ruth's story conjures a vision of ethnic and cultural harmony through the house of David, which claims her as a direct ancestress."[4]

This Bible study explores the story of three women to critique how we are kept apart as peoples—by intentionally created systems of "divide and rule"—not unlike my friend Qamar from Pakistan and her friends here in India! A feminist critique of historical divisions and borders ought to help us to move to another realm of relationship which refuses divide but rather forges bonds of unity and solidarity among us as women and men within nations and across the continents, overcoming many historical obstacles in our way. I will situate this ancient biblical narrative in the context in today's realities and identify its potential to challenge oppressive systems that have ensured that some women and men are kept in a situation of discrimination based on region, country, class, race, caste, sexual orientation and ability.

I have been told that it is not helpful to keep looking back at past history, and that it is more important to critique and work against present systems of economic and political injustice, patriarchy, caste and race. While I will not contest the need to act in the present, my concern is that if we do not situate the present context in a past history that systematically and intentionally created injustices and divisions between us, we cannot deal with present injustices nor can we build unity which is the core mandate that we have been given as Christians. Colonialism and what followed as neocolonialism and the present phase of globalisation that has gone with it are in a continuum—one flows into the next, and sometimes overlaps—but all have buttressed processes of divisions among nations and between peoples. There is also exploitation and plunder of the wealth and resources of some nations which contributed richly to the wealth of a handful of "occupying" or colonising nations and the undermining of the knowledge systems, ways of life and livelihood of some peoples.

A postcolonial reading of the text is a way to liberate the text and empower us in our engagement with each other to find alternative communities of solidarity and power.

It is important to reread the book of Ruth from the perspective of women who have survived extreme poverty and institutionalised systems of social and cultural discrimination—of patriarchy, caste, race and identity. It is only recently that liberation theologians such as Dalit theologians in India recognised that their theologies are incomplete if they do not take into account the doubly and even thrice oppressed women in their communities.[5]

Finding a Home for "the Other" among Asian Women

"For these converts, who were mainly outcastes and Tribals (a word with which the Indigenous peoples in South Asia identify themselves) their principal encounter with the colonial power was through the mission agencies and their welfare work. They were the recipients of the beneficent effects of missionary work.... They saw their dignity being restored by the intervention of missionaries and colonial administration in cases like the Upper Cloth Movement in Travancore."[7] Dr. B.R. Ambedkar, who is considered the father of the Dalit Movement and one of the writers of the Indian Constitution, strongly advocated conversion as a weapon against the upper castes "whenever they (the Dalits) have been subjected to limits of their endurance in the area of social discrimination as well as economic exploitation."[8]

The continuing hesitation of the churches in South Asia to respond to women's legitimate claims has been unfathomable. Solidarity among women does not come easily—we are kept apart by social, cultural and economic forces. The solidarity between Naomi and Ruth informs us as we try to build bonds of solidarity across this subregion. And for Orpah... do we need to find a home for her too?

A postcolonial reading of the book of Ruth pushes the boundaries. It challenges us as women to not just depatriarchalise the biblical texts but also decolonise them. Orpah stays back with her ancestors; most commentaries do not devote more than a sentence to her or sometimes even draw attention to her as the one who opts for freedom from responsibility when she leaves her mother-in-law.

"Staying back" is here a politically charged concept. To stay on the land when Orpah could have escaped to another place seems to be her choice. Looking at her choice through Native American eyes, Laura Donaldson says that Orpah's action denotes quite the opposite. "To Cherokee women, for example, Orpah connotes hope rather than perversity, because she is the one who does not reject her traditions or her sacred ancestors. Like Cherokee women have done for hundreds if not thousands of years, Orpah chooses the house of her clan and spiritual mother over the desire for another culture."[9] This would be true of Indigenous peoples in all our countries who are being literally forced to move out of their ancestral homes—made illegal and hounded out wherever they go. For many communities of people, ancestral lands have a deep spiritual connect with their lives (even when they have given up their ancestral gods and opted for Christianity or other religions). Choices such as what Orpah made are not always readily available to Indigenous peoples today given the power of the globalisation of labour, the denial of land rights (see, for example, the struggles of the Palestinian people against the illegal occupation of their lands) and the economic dependency of the majority of the peoples of the earth. The point made here by Donaldson is valid. Orpah's courage to go back to her ancestral gods and culture is no small feat and ought to be commended in any rereading of the text.

Finding a Home for our Solidarity with Women and Men Across the Globe

The point I wish to make in this Bible study is that colonial relationships affect our contacts as women in this South Asian region itself and also as Christians around the world, as our social locations and the political and economic interests of our nations take precedence over our common humanity and, more importantly, our common heritage as the community of women and men in Jesus Christ. Systematically and intentionally the solidarity among us as the Naomis, Ruths and Orpahs of today has been broken by economic interests, religious interests, caste interests and even gender and sexual identities.

The Word of God in this text: Ruth, Naomi and Orpah as a Perfect Example of Solidarity!

The Book of Ruth, however, affirms the solidarity between these women, even with a level of manipulation which was the only political tool they had available to them to survive. (Remember the episode in Chapter 3 where Ruth deceives Boaz into marrying her—aided and abetted by her mother-in-law!) The potential of joint strategies and joint actions for the sake of the liberation of all women and men is something we ought not to give up too easily, especially in a context of economic globalisation and empire when economic, political and social forces are engineering discrimination and injustice within each of our nations and between us as women of various religious persuasions around South Asia. The story of Naomi, Ruth and Orpah is a story that affirms the power that we celebrate as we seek new ways to forge unity among us for justice and peace. I conclude with these words of hope from Jesus, "I give you a new commandment, that you love one another. Just as I have loved you, you should love another. By this everyone will know that you are my disciples, if you love one another." (John 13:34-35)

Discuss in groups

- What would you say, in your experience, are the forces that hinder solidarity among people today?

- Discuss the significance and challenge of Jesus' new commandment "love one another as I have loved you."

- What would you do to forge unity with those who you would normally have nothing to do with?

Endnotes

[1] Laura E. Donaldson. "The Sign of Oprah: Reading Ruth through Native Eyes," *Hope Abundant: Third World and Indigenous Women's Theology*. Ed. Kwok Pui Lan, (New York: Orbis Books, 2010), 141.

[2] All quotations from the Bible are taken from The New Revised Standard Version of the Bible.

[3] Isabel Apawo Phiri. *Ruth. African Bible Commentary*, Tokunboh Adeyemo, General Editor. (Zondervan, Word Alive Publishers, Kenya, 2006). 319.

[4] Laura E. Donaldson 143.

[5] *Dalit Theology in the Twenty First Century: Discordant Voices, Discerning Pathways*. Eds. Sathianathan Clarke, Deenabandhu Manchala and Philip Vinod Peacock, (Delhi/Geneva: Oxford University Press and WCC Publications, 2010.)

[6] One such example is referred to the "Breast Cloth or Upper cloth movement", when in the mid-19th century, the missionary movement in the former Travancore state—now part of Tamil Nadu—supported the Chanar women in their struggle to cover their breasts. Till then this had been the privilege of the upper caste Nair women only. For more information on this and on other ways in which the London Missionary Society worked

for the liberation of women, see Joy Gnanadason, *A Forgotten History: The Story of the Missionary Movement and the Liberation of the People in South Tranvancore* (Chennai: Gurukul Lutheran Theological College and Research Institute, 1994).

[7] R. S. Sugirtharajah. "Complacencies and Cul-de-Sacs, Christian Theologies and Colonialism," *Postcolonial Theologies. Divinity and Empire*, Catherine Keller, Michael Nausner and Mayra Rivera eds. (Chalice Press: St. Louis Missouri. 2004) 27

[8] Peniel Jesudason Rufus Rajkumar quoting Lancy Lobo, Dalit Identity and Politics: Cultural Subordination and the Dalit Challenge, "The Diversity and Dialectics of Dalit Dissent and Implications for Dalit Theology and Liberation," *in Dalit Theology in the Twenty First Century*, 58.

[9] Laura Donaldson. *The Sign of Oprah: Reading Ruth through Native Eyes,* 148

Bible Study 2

Becoming a Transformed and Transforming Ecclesia

Text: Luke 13:10-17

In a corner of our newspapers each day there are reports of some incidence of violence against women....

A horrifying case of sexual harassment reported. The police have arrested four people in connection with the case while the prime accused has confessed there are more people involved. The case involves gang members who used to befriend women on social media websites luring them to meet them and then forcefully shooting videos of the women and selling them. Such stories dot our newspapers along with stories of rape, domestic violence—women as targets of violence is an everyday incident in our news channels and newspapers. In such a context how can we become a transformed and transforming community of women and men? What does the Bible have to offer as inspiration to us?

I have chosen to concentrate on a New Testament text for this Bible study on becoming a "Transforming and Transformed Ecclesia." It is one of my own favourite texts in the Bible. The New Testament text gives us a powerful image of the task and role of Christians in South Asia today. The search for the role and vocation of the Asian church encounters us again and again as we struggle as minority communities in all South Asian countries. It is increasingly becoming difficult for minority communities to live in peace in our countries.

We are constantly confronted with the challenge to be a transforming and transformed community nurtured by a deep commitment to make an impact on our countries, of which we are so proud, while keeping the integrity of our faith and witness—without which we would perish as a community. What parable do we need for our times that will challenge us to be ever alert to our calling to be the church of Jesus in all situations and for all people in our national contexts?

In Eerdman's Commentary on the Bible, the writers say that in this text Jesus is not annulling the traditional Sabbath but rather reinterpreting the function of that holy day. At the midpoint of Luke's Gospel, Jesus enters the synagogue for the last time (see Lk 4:31-237; 6:6-11). Mark wrote that "the sabbath was made for humankind, but not humankind for the sabbath," (Mk.2:27) a saying that Luke omitted, perhaps as too critical of a well-known holy day. Jesus argues, in this text, not about whether one should observe the Sabbath, but about the meaning of the day. Jesus "does good" to the crippled woman on the Sabbath, a woman who had a "spirit of weakness" (Mk. 13:11) which may refer to an evil spirit.[1]

The Encounter between Jesus and a Crippled Woman

The event happened in the context of Jesus teaching at the synagogue on the Sabbath day, a day set apart for worship and prayer. The Bible tells us that this woman had been crippled for 18 years with a spirit which debilitated her. She was bent over and could not stand up straight, we are told. This could have been a physical ailment … many with physical ailments did come to Jesus for healing. But this could also be a woman "crippled in her heart" because of a hard life. If it is a physical ailment, imagine for a minute what it would be like to be always bent over, to see the world from the view that a bent-over person has. Such persons will inevitably have a low self-image of themselves as all they can really see is the ground and the feet of others! Today we see the many "bent over" women of our country—women bent over by poverty, by prejudice because they are Dalits or Adivasis, by their age, their sexuality and sexual preferences, their religion, etc. Too many women in South Asia are also bent over by violence they experience in the apparent security of their home, society and even in the church. They are bent over and really cannot stand up straight.

The crippled woman in the Bible story has a strange experience that Sabbath day. Jesus happens to be at the synagogue. **He calls out to her** and sets her free from her ailment. In verse 12 we read, "When Jesus saw her, he called her over and said, 'Woman you are set free, from your ailment.'" Is it not a fascinating fact that she does not ask to be healed—he takes the initiative and calls out to her? Perhaps she is too afraid to come forward for Jesus' healing touch—her bent-overness has made her afraid and hesitant and her self-esteem is so low that she does not even think she is worthy of healing. But Jesus "sees" that she is suffering and invites her to be healed. He lays his hands on her and she immediately stands up straight and her first act, the Bible tells us, is that she began praising God.

Jesus cares for the women of South Asia, for the women of the world. He calls out to us; he weeps with us in our tears; and seeks us out for his healing touch. This is the central message of this text.

The reaction of the leaders of the synagogue, the church leaders of those times, is strange but perhaps typical for the institutionalised church (v 14). They are indignant that Jesus has healed on the Sabbath and therefore they try to keep the crowds away. They cannot believe that Jesus is breaking the rules on the holy day of the Jews when no work is allowed by law. They refer back to what is familiar, to the rules and regulations, to the traditions that have governed them for centuries (v 14).

But to Jesus all this was irrelevant; what was important was the human life he was saving. To the allegations of the leader of the synagogue, Jesus' response is harsh and perhaps angry. "You hypocrites," he calls them (v 15). If you can care for your ox or your donkey on the Sabbath day, then does not this woman deserve to be set free after 18 years of being bound, he asks. What strong words Jesus uses—"you hypocrites." Sometimes one wishes that Jesus would come into our midst today and would chastise the church and its leaders—women and men—that is you and me, with words as strong as these to awaken us out of our apathy. So often we as a church refer to our past traditions, to structures of governance, to committees and other processes before we will act. Or we will refer to the culture of our society as an excuse for our inaction, for our hypocritical attitudes.

Another significant detail is that Jesus calls this woman "a daughter of Abraham" (v. 16)—he is including her into the genealogy, which is by and large built on a male line. By this Jesus is giving her dignity; she is not just some nobody, she is important, she is a child of God who deserves to be acknowledged, to be healed, so that she can claim her dignity and be able to boldly praise God. Jesus does the unthinkable, he is breaking the law, he has the courage to defy the leaders of the synagogue and to stand for justice, for truth and for the fullness of life. By his courageous action, we are told that his opponents are put to shame, and the entire crowd rejoices at the wonderful things that Jesus is doing. (v. 17)

How often in the Bible we read of such strong words and actions by Jesus. He seems to always be speaking up for the "small ones" in his society. He seems to always recognise those who do not count or are told they do not count. He gives them dignity by drawing them into his community. We remember the woman who was to be stoned to death for being caught in adultery (John 81-11); the Samaritan woman who was considered an outcast in her community (John 4:2-12); the haemorrhaging woman who considered herself unclean (Math. 9:18-26); the paralytic man (Math. 9:2-7); the blind men (Math. 9:27-31); and many more. Jesus' healing touch reaches out to all those who were considered outcasts, to sinners, all who are judged and condemned by human society. In the ecclesia of Jesus (in the Jesus community) no one is rejected, everyone finds a place.

Here we are speaking of a transformed and transforming community of women and men in the church, the eccelsia. What images of the church do we get from this encounter between Jesus and the bent-over woman?

a) **The church as a healing community**: Do we see ourselves as a community that can provide healing to all those with a broken spirit, all those bent over by injustice, by prejudice, by violence. Is the church welcoming to those who have nowhere else to turn? The Dalits, the young, the poor, the unemployed, the addicts, people of diverse sexualities, the women who experience domestic violence or other forms of discrimination—what has been our role as women in our church and society?

b) **The church as a caring community**: Is not the church too often more concerned with its institutional life, with its ministerial structures, with its traditions, with its own survival rather than with its responsibility to be a voice of compassion in our countries and in the world? Are we not too often so inward looking that we do not see our role in the world—to be the voice of those who are unable to speak out? Do we not, as women in churches, prefer to be like the crippled woman, hide from public view rather than to claim our rightful place and to speak out with courage when things are going wrong in the church and society? In India an amazing and unseen movement began in the end of December—literally hundreds of Muslim women came out of their homes, their often secluded lives, to join protests in all the major cities of the country against a new law that threatened to render a large majority of their community stateless. Many of them told us they were not doing this for themselves (fearful as they are) but for the protection of the secular fabric of India's Constitution and society! The question I was asked a few days ago haunts me—would Christian women come out and protest as the Muslim women were doing?

How can we and our churches become transformed and transforming communities and reach out and touch such people and draw them into the circle of caring and love? These are all questions we need to ask ourselves because the ecclesia of Jesus can only be a caring community.

c) **The church as an inclusive community**: We live in a world that excludes large sections of people. Asia is often said to be a region that is on the move. We have some of the fastest growing economies of the world. Ironically we now have the capacity to exploit poorer countries, in Asia and in Africa! In the present context of economic globalisation, we cannot forget that in our region itself there are millions poor than there are those, like us, who enjoy the benefits of globalisation. Our comforts are often built on the back of the poor who are systematically excluded from the benefits of economic growth.

We can no longer speak of marginalisation—this does not explain the exclusion that so many people experience. It does not explain the exclusion many Dalits and Indigenous communities feel in our countries. It does not explain the exclusion that millions of women feel in society and in the church. The church has to project a different model of community; if we are to take Jesus' ministry as our model then indeed no one must be excluded. But are we faithful to this? Do we not exclude some because of their gender, age, caste, or community difference or because of their sexual orientation?

The community of Christian women that we represent is one of those groups that feel they have sometimes been excluded from the mainstream social, economic and political life. It is a community that knows the pain that exclusion can bring. Then the question we have to ask ourselves is what kind of responsibility do we have to model on that which celebrates the inclusion of all? How can we as a community of Christian women demonstrate that all are welcome here as part of the Jesus community—that no one will feel judged, condemned or excluded?

d) The church as a risking community: To Jesus, the woman's life and well-being transcended the powers and principalities that set the rules and laws. He challenged them with courage. He condemned their limited and limiting attitudes with strong words. He was well aware of the consequences of his actions, the risks he was taking. We know what the powers did to him at the end—they crucified him because they could not deal with the challenge of his message or his insolent courage. But he was willing to take that risk even unto death. Will we be a risking community in our counties, being ready to speak truth to power however risky that is? Will we as women leave our comfortable corners in the church and step out and speak out in the world?

The Bible is replete with stories of men and women who were willing to take a risk to stand up for the truth in defence of life. Let me remind you of the two midwives in the Exodus story (Ex.1: 15 following). Shiprah and Puah, who risk their lives in order to save the lives of the Hebrew babies. In the only form of resistance open to them they allow the babies to live and defy the power of the mighty Pharaoh, who has ordered them to kill the baby boys. I recollect Queen Vashti, who defied King Ahasuerus and refused to allow her beauty to be used, and Queen Esther, who indeed used her beauty in defence of her people (Esther Ch. 1). Both were women of power who courageously defied authority and arrogant might in standing up for justice and truth.

Are we as a church ready to take risks? Do we not more often prefer to take a line of safety, hiding behind our institutional power, or our minority status, as a church, rather than speak up when we should? Do we not so often prefer to speak of our ministry as a spiritual journey to assure us life after death rather than as a spirituality for life, for the struggle for justice and peace in our world today? It is sometimes too risky to speak of the church as a moral community which has the courage to be "fools for Christ" (I Cor. 4:10), as Paul called us to be. We must be ready to take the challenge to expose the injustice in our world, even if it means putting our own lives and the lives of our communities at risk.

In Christ there is hope. Indeed, if we live with courage and are willing to be a caring and inclusive community. Then the world will see us and rejoice, as the text reminds us. It is this that the world looks to us for—for the model we live out, for our courage to be faithful to our calling. To be a church that takes risk is indeed difficult, it demands a "sacrificial lifestyle," which Paul describes as the major quality of discipleship (Romans 12:1). But in this we have the assurance of companionship, of Jesus' compassionate love and of the abundance of life. The Jesus who heals on the holy day, the Sabbath, offers us that healing and acceptance today. Let us have the courage to submit to that invitation.

Part II: Working with the Text: (an action)
Women for Transformation: Potential and Challenges

This text of healing and of transformation leads us to becoming a transformed community. We are healed and therefore can be healers. We are made to stand up straight (even when we do not ask for it) and therefore have the ability to ensure that other women and men can also stand up straight and we can together praise God. **Christ comes to us women today!** This we believe in, that Jesus accompanies us women in our everyday experiences of life and in our struggles to find justice and a violence-free world. It is a faith that knows no boundaries, a faith that sustains us in our struggles for life. Jesus is that theology of life—God with us.

Stand in a circle and bend over and stay bent over till the leader of the group touches a few persons and helps them stand up straight—then those who are upright touch others and help them stand up straight. Do this slowly and with deep conviction of truly helping each other. After everyone stands upright discuss the following questions in groups:

1. What did you experience when you were bent over? What did you see?

2. Share the story of someone you know who is bent over. How does she/he relate to God?

3. Who are the bent-over in South Asian society? Name the groups of people who are bent over? Discuss why they are bent over.

4. What will I do in my church/community when I go back home to help other women and men stand upright?

5. How does this story relate to your image of a transformed church in South Asia?

Have a brief session of reflecting together on the questions. The leader can ask a few persons or representatives from some of the groups to share their discussions with the whole group.

Women Celebrating Church as Event

Invocation

O that you would tear open the
Heavens and come down
So that the mountains would quake
At your presence

Bow your heavens, O Lord, and come down.

Breathe into our bones afresh
Wind from the North and the South,
From the East and the West.
Give us a new flesh, a new spirit, a new heart.

Song: Sung by the congregation or music by drums (a song chosen by the context/region)

A Meditative Reading: The congregation sits silently (The leader can ask the group to close their eyes and breathe in and out for a minute).

Reader: A Time for Birth

A time for birth
Yet so much of birth is waiting:
a seed planted in the earth, slowly taking root;
an idea, moment of inspiration, slowly taking shape;
a talent, hardly guessed at, slowly unfolding;
a love, scarcely noticed, slowly maturing;
a child, original creation, slowly forming.
So much of birth is waiting, in darkness,
It cannot be hurried, this time for birth.

And then, suddenly, I am outraged by pain,
tearing my flesh, tearing my soul,
battering all my resistances,
pulling down all my defences.

I must embrace this?
I had not thought that co-operating with life's rhythms
Would hurt so much.

Nothing ever turns out the way you imagine,
But slowly, painfully, I am learning to trust
The wisdom of birth.

In the uncertainty of waiting, God was.
And I see now, it was good.

In the new life being born, God was.
And I see now, it was good.

In giving birth, I see I too am changed
a new creation,
and it is good.

The wisdom of birth is God's gift to me,
And my gift to the world.

I give great thanks.

(by Kathy Galloway, who was leader of the Iona Community, Scotland)[1]

Confession
Let us confess
The secret sins in the hidden spaces of our lives
Which hold us in fear and anguish,
Keeping us from God and each other.

Silence

Let us confess
the words of judgement which we should have spoken
the compromises we have made which allow evil to multiply
producing harvests of destruction and death.

Silence

Let us confess
the complacency with which we live in disunity
the ease with which we keep our prejudices
refusing to be the one people of God for which Jesus prayed

Silence

Response (spoken together)
God from whom nothing is hidden
and who knows the motives of our hearts
forgive us our sins
and declare to us the joyful truth
and we are a liberated people. Amen

Meditative Reading followed by three minutes of silence
We are women waiting restlessly
As a liberated people in the love of God
Contemplating the contours
Of Church as event
Planning, organising, resisting all that blocks or distorts our
vision
Calling for unity, for solidarity
Waiting for the birth of new life
A new church, a new world

The following text from Luke's Gospel is read out slowly
even as all are sitting or kneeling (as they are able):

"And Mary said:
'My soul magnifies the Lord,
And my spirit rejoices in God my Saviour,
For he has been mindful of the humble state of his servant.
From now on all generations will call me blessed,
For the Mighty One has done great things for me.
Holy is his name.
His mercy extends to those who fear him,
From generation to generation.

He has performed mighty deeds with his arm;
He has scattered those who are proud in their inmost
thoughts.
He has brought down rulers from their thrones
But has lifted up the humble.
He has filled the hungry with good things
But has sent the rich away empty.
He has helped his servant Israel,
Remembering to be merciful to Abraham
And his descendants forever, even as he said to our fathers."'

ALL: My soul magnifies the Lord.

Reflection

In Luke 1:46-55 we read Mary's song of praise to God. Mary's song flows unpremeditated from her heart. Her words are her spontaneous response upon being pronounced as blessed by her relative Elizabeth, the expectant mother of John the Baptist.

But that is just the immediate setting in which we find Mary's song. We would be wise to also keep in mind the larger context in which Mary spoke these words. It was a time of great uncertainty, for Mary faced a bleak future.

Thus, in the words of Rev. Carolyn Sharp, "Don't envision Mary as the radiant woman peacefully composing the Magnificat." Instead see her as "a girl who sings defiantly to her God through her tears, fists clenched against an unknown future." When we do this, Rev. Sharp goes on to say, "Mary's courageous song of praise [becomes] a radical resource for those seeking to honour the holy amid the suffering and conflicts of real life."[2]

Hearing afresh Mary's message

Normally when we read or listen to Mary's *Magnificat*, we're tempted to soften its message and spiritualise its meaning. But I would like for us to read Mary's song afresh, as if for the first time. As we do so, let us ask why so many have understood Mary's message to be subversive and revolutionary.

The Messiah that Mary anticipated is referred to as the Mighty One who topples rulers, scatters the proud, and sends the rich away empty-handed. However, he is also mindful of the lowly, exalts the humble, fills the hungry with good things.

In other words, Mary anticipates that the Messiah will bring about "wondrous reversals" in the world, to borrow Rev. Carolyn Sharp's phrase. Mary envisions God's anointed one upsetting the status quo by turning virtually everything upside down. He is one who inverts human structures and values. After all, God chose for him to be born of a "lowly servant girl" instead of a woman of prominence.

So picture this with me, if you will: There sits Mary, attempting to recover from the long trip to Bethlehem and the stressful conditions in which she gave birth to Jesus. As she stared up at the night sky and undoubtedly saw Herod's luxurious resort, what thoughts do you think entered her mind?

Time for your input

When you read Mary's *Magnificat*, what sort of Messiah do you see Mary anticipating? Before reading this reflection, have you ever considered Mary's song to be subversive?[3]

Consider the Magnificat in the context of Church as Event. It calls for a community united in transforming unjust structures, of speaking truth to power, of challenging patriarchal power structures that interrupt women's efforts to create a new reality for the people of the world. Of giving voice to those who have been rendered powerless.

ALL: My soul magnifies the Lord.

Intercessory prayer

Let us pray:

Where ignorance, self-love and insensitivity
Have fractured lives in community,
Give us hearts that care, O God of love

Where injustice and oppression have broken
The spirit of peoples,
Give us hearts that propel us to action, O God who frees

Where hunger and poverty, illness and death
Have made life an unbearable burden
Give us hearts that challenge our apathy, O God of grace

Where suspicion and hatred, division and conflict
Have challenged your goodness
Give us hearts filled with the longing for justice, O God of peace.

Eternal God

Our mother and our father

Open our eyes and the eyes of our leaders

So that the nations in our region may walk in the light of love

Remove ignorance and stubbornness, intolerance and hatred from our nations

So that we may work together with diligence and determination

for your peace, justice and love.

Amen

Blessing

God of power,

May the boldness of your Spirit transform us

May the gentleness of your Spirit lead us,

May the gifts of your Spirit

Equip us to mould ourselves and all the spaces we meet together in

and all we work with to create Church as Event in all we do!

Now and always.

Amen

Poems, Prayers, Worship Resources

A prayer

Let us pray:

Jesus, come to us women today,

Celebrate along with us our small victories.

A poem we will write together, rather than spend endless times weeping.

A song of liberation we will sing

As we become together a transforming and transformed ecclesia.

A theology of resurrection we will write together, as we deconstruct all that is unjust.

A dance of freedom we will dance,

Dancing away all that creates disharmony and causes us rage.

Christ come to us women today.

And promise to walk this journey with us.

Christ come to her, my sister, today,

Weep with her as she weeps tears of pain,

A poem of love, write for her, and remind her that God cares.

A song of liberation, sing for her, challenging her to reclaim her power to struggle.

A theology of resurrection write for her, empowering her to refuse the theology of sacrifice.

A dance of freedom dance with her, giving her the strength to stand up and dance with you.

Jesus come to us women today

Promise to walk that journey with us.

Jesus come to the church today,

Weep for her, for her lack of courage and strength

A poem of love, write for her to remind her of your passion and love.

A song of liberation, sing to her to awaken her to your message of your salvation even in this cruel world

A theology of resurrection, write for us when you called on us to live in right and just relationships.

A dance of freedom, dance with us challenging us to stand up and dance for you.

Christ, come to the church today

Promise to walk that journey with us. Amen. (Aruna Gnanadason)

Privilege

Christina Thomas Dhanaraj[*]

There is no beauty in this ugliness; no, none at all.

There is no beauty in standing next to you, shoulder to shoulder, and see someone else holding your hand.

It is not cathartic to tell a story of brokenness, of vulnerability, to an audience white with privilege.

It is not romanticized history that I carry on my back, I show through my scars, and I sing about in my songs.

I'm not exotic.

I'm not beautiful; especially not because of my pain.

There's no beauty in waiting, wanting, and losing.

And there's no joy in chasing.

There's absolutely no romance in breaking within or breaking up.

There's no magnificence in shame.

So don't come to me because you think I'm exotic; don't come to me because you think my pain is my beauty.

---

*Christina Thomas Dhanaraj is a third-generation Christian Dalit woman from Bengaluru, India. She holds a Master's degree from the National University of Singapore and currently works as a business analyst. She believes all of us have a story to tell, and none of us should be ashamed of it. She enjoys theatre, as well as writing poetry and microfiction. She was most recently part of the Dalit history month collective (Dalithistory.com). Madrasmag – **Published: 05/08/2015. With the author's permission.**

My vulnerability is not my seduction; and it will never be your triumph.

Your eyes, they have to stop seeing me the way they do; with pity and helplessness.

My ancestors who broke their back and sacrificed their lives, who spoke of you with utter disgust, didn't die in vain.

They warned me of you, and I'm warning you now; stay away and don't come near.

Don't talk to me like you know me; don't fucking specimenize me.

I owe you no conversation, I owe you no friendship.

I will deprive you of the space you stole from my people; I will not adjust to let you speak.

But most importantly, mind you, I will fuck your privilege, and I will fuck it good.

Children: The Unfinished Agenda!

"They are like that. One must not hold it against them. Children should always show great forbearance towards grown-up people." The Little Prince, Antoine de Saint-Exupéry, 1944.

Remember the millions of children in South Asia and all over the world as they live in daily contexts of violence or under the shadow of war. I wonder how they perceive our anxieties as adults as we reflect on the situation in our world. I think of some of the questions that children should rightfully ask us, adults, at this time and think too of the ways in which we sometimes so carelessly (or perhaps helplessly) answer them.

What shall we tell our children when they ask why everything in their world seems to be going wrong?

Shall we tell them not to worry…that everything will be set alright, eventually?

What shall we tell those children who live in a context of deprivation—daily worrying about food, clothing and shelter?

Shall we tell them that this is life and that they should thank God for the small blessings that they enjoy?

What shall we tell a child whose father has just been retrenched because the public sector is being closed down and whose mother's low-paying job cannot get enough food on the table?

Shall we tell her to give up her education and look out for work?

What shall we tell the child who lives on the streets and lives dangerously, expecting some form of violence every night?

Shall we tell her to be patient, and if she works hard and is not lazy, that she will get a break someday?

What shall we tell a child who is lured into prostitution, is then trafficked from one country to another and who longs for her family and her childhood?

Shall we tell her to wait till she grows up, because then she can fight for her legal, economic and social rights?

What shall we tell a child who watches her mother being beaten by her father, or being driven out of their home in his drunken rage?

Shall we tell her not to take this seriously because there are much graver forms of violence in the world?

What shall we tell a child who sees her people being discriminated against because of their race, their Dalit-ness, their Adivasi origins or their ethnic identity?

Shall we tell her to overlook such discrimination and hope that she will be one of the few lucky ones who may just make it in an unjust world?

What shall we tell a child who is sexually abused by someone she trusts and looks up to—a parent, a teacher, a caregiver or even a clergyman?

Shall we tell her not to exaggerate, or to remain silent, because no one will believe her anyway?

What shall we tell a child who is taught that her religion is the right way and that all others worship false gods?

Shall we teach her to remember this always and to grow up with a sense of arrogant triumphalism rather than with thankfulness for the rich plurality that God bestows on us?

What shall we tell the child who ask us where all the clean air, the many diverse forms of fauna and flora, the sparkling streams, the sandy beaches and beautiful snow-capped mountains are slowly disappearing to?

Shall we tell her not to care, but to continue to live life to the full, and watch silently as we extract more and more from the resources of the earth?

What shall we tell those children who are made to believe that their nation is strong and that war is the only way in which peace can be achieved and justice won?

Shall we tell them to stay calm and not fear the future, knowing full well that those preparing for war are unable to guarantee their security?

What shall we tell an Indian child who asks us about Pakistan, when will she be able to visit her Muslim friend who has moved there with her family?

Shall we tell her not to think of this as they are our "enemies" whom we just have to destroy?

What shall we tell a child who asks us why some children beg on the streets, do not go to school but work as daily wage labourers?

Shall we tell her that our country has no money to care as the national priority is on arming ourselves in case we are attacked?

What shall we tell our children when they ask why some wars are considered just and other wars are seen as unacceptable?

Shall we tell them to not care about such matters—knowing that we live in a world of grave injustice, where the powerful call the shots and believe they have the right to make such claims?

What shall we tell our children when they ask why they cannot play with toy guns or with video games that teach them how to kill or to target tall buildings, while the news on the TV shows them adults doing just that with real guns and real planes?

Shall we tell them to just listen to us because as adults we know what is right for them and what is wrong?

What shall we tell those children who are not allowed to go out and play, because they could be the targets of a stray bullet, a landmine or a cluster bomb?

Shall we tell them that one day the world may be a safer place for them?

What shall we tell our children who are made to watch their mothers being raped, fathers shot to death or brothers abducted and forcibly enlisted into armies?

Shall we tell them not to be traumatised, that life has to go on and that they will outlive their pain and terror?

What shall we tell the child who is enlisted into an army and is made to carry a gun and is taught to kill or maim or to rape and pillage?

Shall we tell him to put his weapon down and get a decent life?

What shall we tell our children who live in tents in refugee camps all their lives?

Shall we tell them that one day they will be free to return to their homeland and to their own homes?

What shall we tell our children when they ask what Christmas is really about?

Shall we have the courage to tell them who the Christ-Child really is and what Christ's presence demands of us—of God with us, ushering in peace and justice, equality and respect—all that the world so desperately needs?

Children have the right to know—the world they live in today is theirs. We have a responsibility to offer them honest answers. But more than that, we have to put an end to all the violence, put an end to all wars, without making any compromises. The children of the world deserve a safe world and a just future. Violence can never be the answer, it can never be the last resort. How can we strengthen the culture of peace with justice for the children of the world? We have so many opportunities to be an alternative and just community.... Will we take up every chance to become valued members of the Jesus community?

Afterword
Birthing a Gender-Just Church in the COVID/Post-COVID-19 Pandemic Era

Kochurani Abraham *

When life comes to a standstill, it is time to raise existential questions. The COVID-19 pandemic has brought the world to a standstill by turning systems of power upside down. The unrelenting tug of war between the forces of life and death unleashed during the pandemic left humans aghast across the globe, as the virus danced around crushing economies besides human health. In the bargain, even superpowers had to taste the bitter cup of vulnerability that has been the everyday lot of the *'Les Misérables'* of this world.

The pandemic, which has turned out to be a history marker, can be a 'turning point'[1] in the unfolding story of humanity. Even amidst the abysmal chaos triggered by the pandemic, the crisis can become a 'turning point' when its life-giving potential is tapped in a way that can transform human life and sustain life on this planet. As noted by I Ching: "After a time of decay comes the turning point. The powerful light that has been banished returns. There is movement, but it is not brought about by force.... The movement is natural, arising spontaneously. For this reason, the transformation of the old becomes easy. The old is discarded and the new is introduced. Both measures accord with the time; therefore no harm results."[2]

The 'old' giving way to the 'new' is a welcome phenomenon as it serves to recreate life in a way that restores its meaning and purpose. It is noted that epidemics hold up the mirror to human beings as to who we really are. That is to say, they obviously have everything to do with our relationship to our mortality, to death, to our lives. They also reflect our relationships with the environment—the built environment that we create and the natural environment that responds. They show the moral relationships that we have toward each other as people, and we are seeing that today.[3]

If the experience of the pandemic poses a 'turning point' challenge for humanity, no institution that has a significant say on life can be spared of its undercurrents.[4] This calls us to revisit the church in its transition from pre-COVID to the post-COVID times and see how it can emerge through this crisis into a compelling and prophetic presence that has a liberative influence on this world.

Gender justice is an area that calls for a critical revisiting in the institutional church with a sense of urgency. Over the last four decades, this issue has been addressed in the ecclesiastical circles at different levels; nevertheless, it is doubtful if these considerations have had a transforming impact on church life. The outward signs of how the church lives out its identity and mission makes apparent the configuration of gender relations and the subsequent power equations within its structures and in its everyday functioning. While certain Christian denominations have taken some steps towards bringing greater gender parity in its pastoral life by sharing sacramental power with women, churches in general continue to uphold religious power as male privilege. Whereas churches declare their mission as care of the least and the lost, there is much incongruence within as women and gender non-conforming persons continue to occupy the margins. The alarming increase in violence against women and girls during the COVID-19 lockdown was termed a 'shadow pandemic' across the globe,[5] and the experiences of Christian women would not be any different on this issue.

A turning point calls for "a new 'paradigm'—a new vision of reality; a fundamental change in our thoughts, perceptions and values," argues Capra.[6] Applying this to ecclesiastical life, it is clear that this demands a determined and consistent rethinking on what it means to be church in theory and praxis. The problematic about the current model is that it is predominantly founded on a clericalised gender hierarchy, where women and others who belong to sexual minority groups occupy the lowest rungs of the ecclesiastical ladder. This gendered positioning denies women and others the right to represent and mediate the divine officially within the ecclesiastical community. Besides, this blocks the church from becoming a credible witness of gender justice to the world.

A gender-just church is a community that affirms and lives the basic dignity and equality of all human persons irrespective of their gender or sexual orientation. Theologically it is founded on the inclusive and egalitarian vision of the reign of God initiated by Jesus Christ. A re-envisioning of ecclesial life that can be a turning point experience for the present church would mean a radical return to two fundamental experiences of the Jesus movement. This implies creating communities which are non-hierarchical and non-clerical.

The question is: why do we need to rethink the church in these lines? The Scriptures make it explicit that Jesus Christ blatantly opposed hierarchical thinking in forming his early community of disciples. The Gospel imperative "It shall not be so among you" (Mt 20:26) is illustrative of the countercultural vision of Jesus, who envisaged the community of his disciples in radically inclusive and egalitarian terms. It is also evident from the Gospels that Jesus did not call himself nor his disciples priests and that his horizons were clearly prophetic. He did not belong to a priestly family and is never shown functioning as a priest in the temple cult. In fact, Jesus vehemently opposed the Jewish structures of priestly domination. Jesus was called a rabbi in his functions as preacher, teacher and exegete in his hometown synagogue (Lk 4:15ff). Clerical priesthood as a necessary condition for Christian leadership is a later development in the historical process of the institutionalisation of the church.

Against the backdrop of the Christian experience that led to the founding of the church, it is important to keep in mind a basic principle that if some models of leadership have evolved in the church in response to certain socio/political and historical contexts, they need to be deconstructed if they become a counter-witness to the original Christian vision and if the changing times demand different structures. Clericalism creates divisions or hierarchical binary structures which can be seen as the strongest characteristic of patriarchal thinking. For Rosemary Radford Ruether, inclusion of women into these structures of clerical power is not the answer but the 'dismantling of clericalism', as a feminist understanding of ministry and clerical ecclesial structures are diametrically opposed to each other.[7]

Making this paradigm shift implies making a major turn from a top-down approach to a democratic ordering of ecclesiastical relationships. This calls for a fundamental change in our perception about God, about ways of being human and a rethinking about spirituality, ministry, leadership and mission.

Gender justice is the new wine that cannot be poured into the old wine skin of a gendered texture and nature. Birthing this new vision of being church is challenge of the hour. For this to happen, we need to engage in more critical conversations about the meaningfulness and urgency of bringing about gender-just relations in the domestic space and in the public sphere. The COVID pandemic challenges us to initiate these conversations once again. The coming into being of a gender-just church could happen in the bargain, though not without the birth pangs.

Endnotes

* **Dr. Kochurani Abraham** is an Indian feminist theologian, researcher, writer and trainer on issues related to gender, sexuality, spirituality and ecology. She has a Licentiate in Systematic Theology from the Pontifical University of Comillas, Madrid, and a PhD in Christian Studies from the University of Madras, India, with a special focus on feminist theology. She was the national convener of the Indian Christian Women's Movement (ICWM), an autonomous movement of Christian women committed to justice concerns in India. At present she is the Vice President of the Indian Theological Association, and is active in Indian Women Theologian's Forum and World Forum of Theology and Liberation. Her book *Persisting Patriarchy: Intersectionalities, Negotiations, Subversions* was published by Palgrave Macmillan New York in 2019.

[1] I borrow the expression 'turning point' from Fritjof Capra's 1983 work *The Turning Point*, published by London: Flamingo.

[2] I Ching cited by Fritjof Capra in the opening pages of *The Turning Point*

[3] Noted historian and professor of History of Medicine, Frank M. Snowden in an interview by Isaac Chotiner. See Chotiner, "How Pandemics Change History" on https://www.newyorker.com/news/q-and-a/how-pandemics-change-history?itm_content=footer-recirc, accessed on 15 May 2020.

[4] Snowden points out that epidemics have not only influenced medical science and public health, but also transformed the arts, religion, intellectual history, and warfare. See Frank M. Snowden, *Epidemics and Society: From the Black Death to the Present*, Yale University Press, 2019.

[5] *Statement by Phumzile Mlambo-Ngcuka, Executive Director of UN Women* https://www.unwomen.org/en/news/stories/2020/4/statement-ed-phumzile-violence-against-women-during-pandemic accessed on 15 May 2020

[6] Capra, *The Turning Point*, xviii.

[7] Rosemary Radford Ruether, 'Women-Church: Emerging Feminist Liturgical Communities' in Norbert Greinacher and Norbert Mette (eds). *Popular Religion*, Edinburgh: T&T Clark, 1986, 75.

9 789388 945776